Title

Tussles

Collected Plays

G. D. Nyamndi

Langaa Research & Publishing CIG
Mankon, Bamenda

Publisher:
Langaa RPCIG
(*Langaa* Research & Publishing Common Initiative Group)
P.O. Box 902 Mankon
Bamenda
North West Region
Cameroon
Langaagrp@gmail.com
www.langaapublisher.com

Distributed outside N. America by African Books Collective
orders@africanbookscollective.com
www.africanbookscollective.com

Distributed in N. America by Michigan State University
Press
msupress@msu.edu
www.msupress.msu.edu

ISBN: 9956-558-54-0

© G. D. Nyamndi 2009
First published 2009

DISCLAIMER

This is a work of fiction. Names, characters, places, and incidents are either the author's invention or they are used fictitiously. Any resemblance to actual places and persons, living or dead, events, or locales is coincidental.

Contents

Things Fall in Place

The Will

The Imprisonment of Sende Ghandi

Preface

Ever since creation, at least in so far as the Judeo-Christian paradigm goes, man has played within the reaches of his own volition. He has also been made to play by forces outside his grasp. Eve played with the serpent in absolute defiance of divine prescriptions. The result was recurrent calamity for her descendants. Even the serpent played with its celestial Nemesis, causing a permanent rift between felicity and duplicity. Man has inherited the ensuing paradoxes and tensions, and burns his earthly stay coming to terms with them.

Today, ritual, dance and festival take up and dramatize our worldview and its inherent throbs. Those modes of intrinsic expression bring to life the essential powers of our sacred places, the sweeping force of our rhythmic sounds, but also the felicitous manner in which we celebrate our being.

But this harmony, time-old and beneficent, is shot through by shafts of western presence, so that these days we can no longer talk about ourselves without also talking about that other whose otherness so colours our view, so directs it, really. This is where the new African dramatist receives his assignment. We call him new because he comes touched with a new mission, one that carries him away from the nihilistic bemoaning of pains inflicted, into the exhilarating vista of therapeutic propositions. He is no longer content with just recording and echoing ills and evils suffered; he must now prescribe healing formulae. That way his place and mission in society are restored to their primordial centrality.

These plays articulate in unique ways my own understanding of the playwright's redemptive attributes. They do not emphasize entertainment only; they reach into the psychology of human relations and individual drives, and intimate responses to occasioned challenges. A playwright is a wide, penetrating mind meandering in society. He detects the drunk before he takes his first drop; uncovers the embezzler even before he lays his hands on the collective holding; steels the masses before the calamities of misrule descend on them; hoists the flag of freedom long before revolutionaries come anywhere near the mast. He uses the play for healing purposes.

This collection groups together four plays written between 1995 and 2006. It opens with *The Bite*, my first ever dramatic experiment. Like much else that prologues the complex experience of inventiveness, this first play relies considerably on lived experience. It therefore has a very strongly psychoanalytical edge to it, fed essentially by the turbulent times of the early 90s in my own personal life. Although the title is used metaphorically, it does carry some literal truth with it, and so does much of the action. In essence, this first play is a *bildungs* drama, not very far away in intention from its novelistic forebears.

Things Fall in Place, the second in terms of composition, is in actual fact a tribute to Chinua Achebe whose work *Things Fall Apart* provides the inspirational thrust to the play. The masquerade performance of traditional ritual and western religion, and the integrated ecstasy resulting from that performance: these are the play's essential argument. I pursue this line of thinking further in *Facing Meamba,* my second novel.

The Will and *The Imprisonment of Sende Ghandi* are just the head and tail of the same coin both in their themes and social statements. Women as one will realize are creatures of high premium in my thinking and worldview. These two plays show their moral strength in environments made insipid by the destructive drives in men; and actually feature them as the alternative agents of orderly existence.

The Bite

(A serio-comic play)

Characters

Abod
Yeza
Lobe, university lecturers
Mola L., Cameroonian visitor from America
Bi, Abod's wife
Tita, Bi's father
Andin, Bi's niece
Lum, Abod's niece
Pa Pulli, Dog owner
Ma Pulli, His wife
Zacharias, Bar Attendant
Nurse
Ladies

Scene 1

In Lobe's office
(He is poring over some work. Enter Abod.)

Lobe
I thought you'd called it off. Five, as you can see.

Abod
Oh no! Lectured till four and got into academic
Discussions with Yeza.

Lobe
Where is he, by the way?

Abod
Cooling off in the canteen.

Lobe
Haven't idled away in your absence. Listen to this.
(Reads)

>   The rolling tanks with echoes of bullets
>   And mad red-capped manhunters…

Abod
Stop. Poetic savvy. Who's it by?

Lobe
Why? Me, of course.

Abod
Announces a muscular shift in your ideological
Stance. The alleluia is gone. Now there is angered
Investigation, pointed accusation.

Lobe
You sound so refreshingly different from my night.

Abod
Another sleepless night?

Lobe
None of my making this time, you can be sure.
I was all comfortable in my blanket, deep in holy sleep.
Then the dogs went barking …howling and barking…breaking
The midnight silence.

Abod

Thieves?

Lobe

Maybe, or some man beating his wife.
There was plenty of I don die oo! in the night air.

Abod

Reminds me, Pinky and Boney are due vaccination this week.

Lobe

He's an unusually rich man today who can feed his family
And still keep two bulldogs.

Abod

Who tells you my wife and children eat their fill?
We take turns at skipping meals for the dogs.

Lobe

Then why keep them? Why cling to a status symbol you've
long been denied?

Abod

Nothing of the sort. Thieves. Thrice in two months they
Came. Carted off everything I had of value: TV set,
Hifi, my wife's jewellery, children's clothes, sundry
Household items. But how do you tell successive
Marauding gangs that there is nothing left in your house to
Be stolen?

Lobe

Put up a notice: "Everything of value has already been
Stolen".

Abod

Would you as a thief take such a notice seriously?

Lobe

I would want to see for myself that everything worth
Stealing had indeed been stolen. And if such was the case
I would want the house owner to explain to me -- at gun-point
of course -- why he allowed the house to be emptied when he
knew
I was still to come.

Abod

That's why I keep Pinky and Boney. They give would-be
Visitors of the night the impression that the house has not
Yet been emptied, even if what is left is just hunger and
Bones.

Lobe

I hope hunger does not drive the dogs into making meat of your
Bones.

Abod

It may not be long before it happens.

Lobe

(*Consulting his watch*)

Almost seven. Where do we stop for a drink?

Abod

It's all up to you.

Lobe

What about the Alliance?

Abod

No objection.

Lobe

Or would you have preferred the Club? It's homelier there
Isn't it? Besides, you can exchange ideas with a few
Opinion-wielders at the counter.

Abod

Not much of a difference either way. Opinion-wielders. Hmmm!
Ball-headed fat bellies. Cup-wielders, for all I know.

Lobe

Not cup-wielders only, those club-goers. They are society
Watchers, men who matter. Their views affect our lives.

Abod

Watchers are not movers. They are the mirage between
Words and action. To them, talking is an end in itself.
The discourse of nothingness.

Lobe

Spare me your incurable bleakness.

6

Abod

The times command it.

Lobe

Just listening to you carries me closer to the gates of hell
And to the Club. Shall we be gone?

Abod

By all means.

Curtain

Scene 2

At the Club

(Abod and Lobe enter conversing. A low makossa tune lingers in the background. Two ladies are seated at a table and looking itchy for action.)

Lobe

Zacharias!

Attendant

Sir!

Lobe

I like that sound. Send up the volume.
(Volume goes up. Lobe does a brisk dance. Cuts eye at one of the ladies who joins him on the floor to a hectic performance. Other lady rises and curtsies before Abod. They too join in. Music ends and they seat themselves down, ladies at their table, the two young men at another table not far away from them. Attendant moves over.)

Attendant

Your choices, Sirs.

Lobe

Great idea. Our throats are burning… The ladies…give them drinks on me. Abod?

Abod

Hmmm. Brandy. Triple shot. Make sure there's a full bottle
On standby.

Lobe

Whisky for me. J&B. I feel in very high spirits today.

Attendant

Right, Sirs.
(Returns with the drinks and serves them).

Ladies

(Raising their glasses, then each in turn)

Thanks so much.

Lobe

Pleasure. *(Smacking his lips as he sips).* Good whisky if ever there
Was one.

Abod

I know you have the tongue for it.
(*Enter Mola L caressing a puppet dog*)

Lobe

Ah! Mola L!

Mola L

Yea men!

Abod

(*Eying the puppet*)
What's that you have there?

Mola L.

Why? That's Braky, my labrador retriever.

Abod

But that's a doll.

Mola L.

(*Energetically*)
No, not at all. I couldn't fly Braky over.
Would have been too much trouble, you know. Plus,
Nobody here would have understood his social
Significance. So I had this scaled-down version of him
Specially made for the trip. He's got a lot of sense, speed
And intelligence. He is my permanent expression of social
Achievement. In America, you know, you have to have a
Dog, a thorough-breed, to articulate your status.

Lobe

Sounds really attractive.

Mola L.

Doesn't only sound attractive. It really *is* attractive.

Abod

You were quite some time in coming.

Mola L

And with reason. What would you have had me hang
Around a barren place like this doing? I had to
Achieve… in America. (*Brief silence*) You know…
American society is built around the galvanizing
Mystique of talent. And I got it, you know.

Zacharias
(To Mola L)

Excuse me, sir.

Mola L
(Ignoring the servant by him)

You know, talent.
That's the magic word.

Zacharias

Your order, Sir.

Mola L.

Ah! Yea! I'll do with a glass of water. I don't know,
You know. I'm on treatment for typhoid. That's the only
Thing this place can give you: typhoid and bad water.
You come in from America fresh like water lily. You've
Been drinking good water, eating good food and breathing
Good air. You feel good, you know. Then this place
Handles you. Monstrosities! Garbage chariots of the gods!

Zacharias

(He's been standing all this while by Mola L with the glass of water).
Here, Sir.

Mola L.

Thank you. Is this tap water, Zacharias?

Zacharias

No Sir. Mineral water...Tangui. We don't serve tap water to members.

Mola L.

See what I mean? If you can't be proud of your water
What else are you left with to be proud of? As the
Saying goes, l'eau c'est le vie. But here it looks
Like l'eau c'est le mort!

Abod

Slogans here are not worth the paper they are written
On. Take this one about health for all by the year...

Lobe

4000.

Abod

Yes, health for all by the year 4000. Why 4000? Why not
Now?

Lobe
There you go again. Government cannot satisfy every
Passing whim. Recognize that it is doing much. See the
Reference hospitals and schools.

Abod
They are on paper.

Lobe
Yaounde, Douala and Buea are realities.

Abod
Health is not an elitist commodity.

Lobe
You can quip, but the evidence is there that government
Is doing its best under very tight circumstances. Where else
In the world has a government done so much, so soon
For so many, with so little?

Mola L.
Are you not mistaking your country for America?
America of the magic word called talent?

Abod
Bizarre vision. Very bizarre vision. We cannot be
Moving forward when everyday around me I see misery
Of a kind my mouth cannot represent. We cannot be
Moving forward when civil servants and the jobless
Knock heads over garbage cans for what dogs and the
Many mad have rejected.

Lobe
Same old, worn-out tune. Did you hear what the IMF
Deputy Director General said the other day? He is an
African like you and me. He cautioned: We cannot
Continue to live like the rich when we are poor.

Abod
Health for all!

Mola L.
By the year 4000!

Abod
Wealth for all!

Mola L.

When I'm dead!

Lobe

You both are just toothless bulldogs. Le caravanne aboie
Le chien passe!

Abod

(Laughing)

Le chien aboie, la caravanne passe!

Lobe

Something like that.

Abod

My wife was operated upon two months ago.
You Lobe, you have not cared to see her; yet you claim
To be a friend. We live in a world of perverted values.

Lobe

I'm awfully sorry. I'll come along with you and
Tender my apologies personally.

Abod

Mola L., keep the American dream alive.

Mola L.

I sure will, you know.

Curtain

Scene 3

In Abod's home

(Enter Abod and Lobe.)

Bi
(Beaming)
Welcome, Lobe. I thought you had forgotten me.

Lobe
(Moves over and embraces her)
I am so ashamed of myself.
I had it in mind to come long before now, but you know how
Roughly the times are handling us.

Bi
The times are bad, I know.

Lobe
How are you feeling?

Bi
Some lingering pains. Healing process, I think. Lum! Lum o
O!

Lum
(From offstage)
Mummy!
(Rushes in).

Bi
Get Uncle Lobe something to drink. You know his choice
Don't you?

Lum
Yes mummy.

Lobe
Abod told me what you went through.

Bi
It was quite an experience. That was the first time I was
Administered anaesthesia.

Lobe
Creepy, I imagine.

Bi

Overpowering! Everything just fades out of memory.
You cease to exist. All the troubles of this world stay
Behind. You just go…go…go…into a world of bliss.
What they do to your flesh is none of your worries. They
Cut you up, rip you open, take you apart in bits and
Pieces. You are all flesh and blood, spirit gone
On a journey of discovery.
Then they patch you all up again. As you come closer back
To this side of hell the pain increases. You cannot
Scream. You cannot move. You must lie there and take
It all. That day when I came round I thought I heard a
Voice saying to me: Bi, you are all right. It's me, your
Man. Abod. Even in my half-conscious state the music
Of those words touched me somewhere deep inside.
When I came round fully I saw Abod. He was sitting at
My bedside, caressing my right hand. (*Starts towards Abod*).
His two eyes, deep, dark and passionate, were searching
My own recovering eyes. It was a moment of powerful
Reunion. Only the pains. I wanted to feel him, hold him.
Pains wouldn't let me do it.

(*Embraces Abod passionately. Lobe looks at Abod in mixed admiration and jealousy.
Abod returns the look in excited appreciation. Andin crashes in*).

Andin
(*Panting*)

Anti!

Bi

What? What has happened?

Andin

Lum!

Bi

What, Lum?

Andin

A dog! A bulldog! Mami Pulli's dog!

Lobe

Oh my God!

Andin

Terrible! Horrible! Lum's leg! A beast! Bulldog! From nowhere!
And pounced on her!

Abod
(*With affected calmness*)

I will not hear of it. Go tell whoever is
Responsible for this joke that I want my daughter back
Here…whole. Do you hear me? Whole.

Bi

Threats won't do. Why don't we go there and see what we
Can do?

Abod
(*Raging*)

I'm not going anywhere. I want my child back here
With me, whole and healthy. (*Exit Lobe and Bi*). Where do
I start? (*Bares his pockets*). There isn't a jot of fuel in that
Cranky ekete; besides, the battery is all run down. It will
Require pushing it up and down the hill five times before it
Grumbles into a snort. As soon as I reach that death
Corridor the nurses will push a 40-item list into my
rich hands: we need gauzes sa, we need spirit, we need plaster
We need syringes, the child needs ATT, antibiotics,
Pain-killers…the anaesthetist doesn't come that easily sa…
Unless you want the stitches done just like that, raw.
No! Now is not the time for things like this.
I'm a real corpse. The peanuts I used to
Receive in the name of wages have been slashed by 70%.
The currency has been devalued by 100% and the standard
Of living has gone hay wire! Bank loan taken before
All these upheavals. Every month I have to borrow 5000 frs
At 30% interest to travel to Yaounde for a 10.000 frs
Overdraft. And with all this they tell me a mad dog has
Cut a hole in my niece's legs. Whoever the dog's owner is
Should get ready for me.
(*Storms out*).

Curtain

15

Scene 4

In an emergency ward
(Lum is on a stool wriggling in pain. A nurse is seated in one corner, her arms folded. Lobe, Bi, Ma Pulli and Pa Pulli are standing around conversing in low tones. Abod marches in.)

Abod
Here, now! What is this I'm hearing? *(Bending over Lum's leg).*
Goodness me! What is this? Where is the man
Responsible for this mess?

Lobe
Abod, can you calm yourself down? You are creating a scene.

Abod
Scene indeed! Where is the owner of that animal? *(Turns round and sees Pa Pulli. Reaches for him but is held by Lobe.)*
If anything happens to this child you will give her back to me.
Am I making myself clear?

Bi
We can do without all these threats.

Abod
Woman, you keep your mouth shut.

Nurse
Enough noise. Now down to more serious business. I have
Examined the wounds. The one on the left leg is quite deep
And will require stitching. We will have to send for the
Anaesthetist, unless you want the stitching done just like that…
Raw.

Pa Pulli
We go take care for dat.

Abod
(Visibly relieved)
You had better.

Ma Pulli
Wich kana balluck dis? Na wich or na weti?

Abod
You should know better.

Nurse

You people are wasting precious time. We need
Perforated plaster. Spirit. Let me see, we need
Syringes, Betaldine yellow, gauzes, 40x40. I have all
These things here so you will not need to go to the
Pharmacy.

Abod

Oh! That's very kind of you.

Lobe

What she means is that she has them here on sale.

Nurse

What did he understand? I am a goat and I eat where I am
Tied. All these items will cost 30.000 frs plus 5000 frs
Dressing fee, that's 35.000 frs in all.

*(Lum utters a deep groan. Nurse shoots out her hand. Everyone exchanges
anguished looks).*

Abod

(In a fresh outburst)

Yes! The nurse has spoken.
(Pointing emphatically to her). She has spoken. Are you all
Deaf? She wants 35.000 frs. 30.000 frs for syringes and
Perforated plaster and betaldine yellow and spirit and
Gauzes. 5.000 frs for dressing fee. 30 + 5: 35. That's
What she wants. Ten, ten, ten, and five, thirty-five. Or this
Child will die and I will have to hire a vehicle to carry the
Corpse home and buy a coffin and dress up the corpse
And feed the mourners and entertain the dance groups
And explain to her mother that she was bitten by a mad
Dog.

Lobe

(Holding Abod)

Are you all right?

Abod

(Wrenching himself)

What do you mean am I all right?
I am as all right as those legs you are seeing there.
Why shouldn't I be all right? My plush limousine is
Waiting outside. I have 500.000 frs on me. I'm all right.

And because I'm all right I will go back home and wait
For my daughter there, whole. (*Storms out screaming*).
Whole! W-h-o-l-e!

Lobe

I've never seen him like this.

Bi

I've seen much worse. He rarely gets angry, but when
He does he is a really ugly sight.

Nurse

My hands are still empty.
(*Lum groans again*).

Bi

Pa, make wuna tak no.

Pa Pulli

Ma pikin, we go tak say weti?

Bi

(*Showing nurse some money*)
My dear sister, you know how
The times are. This is all my food money for the month.
7000 frs. As I am giving it to you my children will
Starve, but what do I do?
(*Hands the money to the nurse who takes it grudgingly*).

Nurse

I am accepting it because of you, otherwise you would
Have carried your child to another place.

Ma Pulli

Wandafu! Na so dog i tit fit cos moni?
(*Receives a scolding look from Pa Pulli*).

Nurse

You are even lucky that the dog was vaccinated.
Here. These are the other drugs she will need.

Bi

God have mercy!

Nurse

These drugs or your daughter's life. The choice is yours.

Curtain

Scene 5

In Abod's house
(He is slumped in a chair. Bi comes in bearing a lengthy prescription.)

Abod
(Angrily)
Where are you from?

Bi
Look, don't ask me stupid questions. *(Derisively)*
Where are you from. If everybody had fled from the
Hospital the way you did, who would have taken care
Of Lum? Do you think it's noise that solves problems?

Abod
Woman, this is no time for trading words. Where is the
Girl and how is she?

Bi
That's the man who claims to be so concerned about his
Daughter's health. Where did you go when you left the
Hospital? If you had come straight here you would have
Seen me bring her back home. She is inside there resting.
Here is the prescription the nurse gave me.
(Hands it to him but he ignores it). Are you not taking it?

Abod
(Grimly)
You were telling me an interesting story. Why don't
You just continue?

Bi
As you like. The nurse says …

Abod
Not the nurse. Noise and problems.

Bi
Abod. All these drugs must be bought and administered
This evening. I stopped at the pharmacy and inquired
About the prices. The five drugs will cost a total of
89.650 frs. The last 7000 frs we had here I surrendered
To the nurse so that she could stitch the wound.

19

Abod

(*Jumping to his feet*)

Now this woman wants to make me
Madder than I am already. How did that piece of
Paper enter your hand? (*Closing in dangerously. Bi steps backwards*).
Out you go! Don't stand there staring at me.
Take that scrap to where it belongs. By the
Way, why have you been so aloof all this evening?
Is it because Lum is not your relative?

Bi

Take it as you please.

Abod

All through the evening you were conversing quietly
With Lobe. And even laughing!

Bi

Me! Laughing! You must be out of your senses.

Abod

There she goes insulting me! What I am going through
Is not bad enough. I must be insulted on top of it!
(*Slaps her*).

Bi

You again using physical violence on me. This is one
Time too many. This is the last straw. From now hence
You can consider this marriage as terminated.
(*Runs out*).

Abod

What do I care? Only make sure that scrap in your hand
Returns to where it came from before you terminate
Anything. (*Mimicking her*) This is one time too
Many…this is the last straw… I don't blame you. You have
Seen your own koko on whom to empty your grammar.
You were bringing me a bill of 89.650 frs… (*Baring his pockets*).
This is as rich as I am. (*Laughing in self-pity*). Abod the
Tycoon! Bring me the prescription! And a lot more!
(*Exits with continued laughter*).

Curtain

Scene 6

In Lobe's office
(He is conversing with Yeza.)

Lobe

Something really nasty has happened to Abod.

Yeza

Quoi par exemple?

Lobe

He has battered his wife again.

Yeza

Abod aussi!

Lobe

An unfortunate incident occurred in his house
Yesterday. A dog bit one of his children.

Yeza

Quoi? Un chien? Pas trop grave, non ?

Lobe

Quite serious, I would say. But the most worrying
Part was our friend's behaviour. He screamed at
Everybody, exercised verbal violence on his wife
And would have strangled the dog-owner if I hadn't
Stepped in to save the bewildered old man.

Yeza

Ça par exemple!

Lobe

Things wouldn't have been that bad if he'd
Stopped at that.

Yeza

Il n'a quand même pas fait pire que ça !

Lobe

Precisely ! The verbal rehearsal in the hospital
Became physical action at home. And come to think
Of it. His wife is still recovering from an operation.
I think their marriage is as good as ended.
(Enter Abod).

21

Abod
(*Morosely*)

Morning you both.

Lobe

Abod, how could you have done this to your wife?

Yeza

Mais dis, il paraît que tu as fait la fête à ta femme hier.

Abod

Ye-za…come on.

Lobe

Your wife woke me up this morning and when I saw
her I thought the little girl had died
During the night or something. I was far from thinking
That you had spent the night trying to kill your own
Wife. You are just a stinking son of a bitch. She has
Made up her mind to quit. I wish you plenty of fun.

Abod

Ouf! What do I care? If she thinks that what happened
To my daughter was not bad enough to warrant my
Outrage, then so be it. I have a right to my anger.

Lobe

Granted, but that anger is not to be vented on surrogate
Victims. Your wife did not commission that dog to bite
Your daughter. After the accident you sat there raving
Idly. It was she who rushed to the scene. All along she
Showed more concern than you. I am thoroughly
Shocked to hear you say she was aloof. What did you
Want her to do? Role on the ground? Tear her clothes
In grief?

Abod
(*With visible regret*)

I hope you put in a kind word for me.

Lobe

I don't condone recklessness. You had your head on
Your two shoulders and you knew what you were
Doing.

Abod

I think you people are blowing it up a bit too much.

22

Lobe

That's as you think.

Yeza

En tout cas, mon cher, cela va se régler entre vous
Deux. Moi je pense surtout aux enfants. Ils sont
Toujours les premières victimes des conneries des
Adultes. Quoi que vous fassiez, ton épouse et toi,
Ne perdez pas de vue l'intérêt des enfants. Lobe,
Pendant que nous y sommes, il va falloir que nous
Mettions en place une stratégie pour sauver ce qui
Peut encore l'être.

Lobe

Abod shouldn't count on me to clean up his mess.

Yeza

Soit. Mais tu sais, c'est bien aussi de temps en temps
De faire en sorte que même ton chien ait peur de toi.
(Laughs).

Lobe

So women have become dogs you can beat at will.

Yeza

Toi aussi. C'est pas ce que je voulais dire. Je voulais
Dire par là qu'il faut savoir se faire respecter de temps
A autre.

Lobe

And you think that torturing your wife is the best way
To command her respect. We will see how much
Respect this one's wife gives him from now hence.

Yeza

Alors là! Ça a l'air plus grave que je ne croyais.
(Enter messenger with note for Abod. He reads it with knowing apprehension).

Abod

(Crestfallen)

It's from my wife. She has left, taking away
All my children.

Lobe

You sowed the wind. Be ready for the tempest.
(Special effects. Loud rumbling sound.)

Curtain

23

Scene 7

In the Club

(Abod, Lobe and Yeza are in conversation.)

Lobe

How did you enjoy your first night as a married bachelor?

Abod

This is nothing to joke about.

Yeza

Ça doit être chouette, non? Une maison à toi tout seul.
Tu sais, les femmes, ça t'empêche souvent de te
Défouler. Je suis sûr que tu es rentré aux petites heures
Du matin.

Abod

I continue to say there is nothing here to joke about.

Yeza

Allons! Ne te fâche pas mon garçon. Je disais ça pour
Plaisanter. Ce qui nous arrive n'est pas drôle du tout.
C'est à prendre très au sérieux.

Lobe

Yes, I think we ought to give serious thought to the
Trend of things. There's certainly a lot more to our
Individual plights than meets the eye.

Abod

Can we be just playthings in some Machiavellian
Hands?

Lobe

There's something deeply wrong in our lives.
Spirit of the times? What the Germans call zeit geist?

Yeza

Tu as dit zeit geist? Je crois que c'est cela.
Nous sommes tous victimes du zeit geist. Notre drame
Existentiel est un signe des temps. La société est en
Pleine dislocation. Les valeurs normatives qui régissent
La cité sont en totale dégénérescence, en chutte libre.

Lobe

Sure. The times are exerting their destructive influence
On us. Society is going to the dogs. Norms have been
Perverted. There is no money. No hope for money.
And yet there is money. We see it on wanton display,
All around us, everyday.

Yeza

Dis, pote, que n'avons-nous pas fait dans la vie pour
Que ceci ne nous arrive pas ? Dix années durant, j'ai
Trimmé pour que plus tard ma famille soit à l'abri de
Tout besoin. Hélas ! Mille fois hélas ! Quand on
M'appelle Monsieur le Professeur je sursaute. Les
Attraits matériels de la profession ont depuis longtemps
Disparu. (*Enter Mola L.*) Ah ! en voilà un qui va sûrement
Nous remonter le moral.

Mola L.

On with the protest song against
Irrationality? Sterile. Absolutely.

Abod

Talking about irrationality, is it normal that
A university lecturer like myself should be forced into
The waiting claws of money-lenders barely one week
After pay?

Mola L.

I don't know you to be an overly extravagant spender.
If your salary cannot keep you going for the month
And still leave you with something to put on the side,
Then, you know, you don't call that a salary. How
Much do you earn, if I may ask. (*The three look at one another in total
embarrassment*). If I'm being
Too indiscrete, we can let it drop. I just thought, you
Know, that we cannot begin to properly x-ray a
Problem if we define it wrongly. Let me put the
Question differently. How much did you use to earn?
Put that way, the question takes better care of your
Lost pride.

Abod

It certainly does, even if the memories it recalls only

25

Torture me all the more. Two years ago I
Earned 450.000 frs a month.

Mola L.

Fair salary, you know.

Abod

Certainly, especially within the specific context
Of the time. Moderate commodity prices, regular
Salary payments, fluid cash flow, minimal
Poverty.

Mola L.

And now?

All three

And now?

Lobe

Abod, tell him.

Abod

From a monthly salary of 450.000 frs two years ago
I have risen to 95.000 frs.

Mola L.

Did you wanna say f-a-l-l-e-n?

Abod

God forbid! Ask our
Gurus and they will prove to you, hand on chest,
That the passage from 450.000 to 95.000 is a
Spectacular climb.

Mola L.

I'm yet to hear something more ridiculous, you
Know, something more insane.

Yeza

Ridicule? Tu as dit ridicule? Il y a fort longtemps
Que le ridicule ne tue plus en Afrique !
(*Laughs*).

Mola L.

I would have expected that from 450.000 two years
Ago, you progress in keeping with the
Upward trend of the cost of living, so that today
Your wage would be in the vicinity of 700.000 frs.
(*All three fall from their seats but recover them immediately*). That

Is what in economics, sound economics, we call
Progressive buying power adjustment, PBPA.

Abod

Your PBPA theory obtains in a sound economy.
Here we practise voodoo economics.
Our up-ended salary increase was followed shortly
Afterwards by a 100% currency devaluation.

Mola L.

And what did the authorities do to alleviate the
Obvious negative consequences of this?

Yeza

Parce qu'ils ont peur de vous?

Mola L.

Without devaluation your monthly wage is
Supposed to be 700.000. Now, if you tell me that
The currency devaluation was 100%, then your
Wage as at the moment of devaluation should have
Been raised by at least 50%, so that you should
Now be earning at least 1.5 million frs a month.
(All three fall again to the floor and remain there. They rise to their feet and vow).

All three

Our money! Our money! It's our money and we
Shall have it!

Lobe

Mola L, thanks for proving to us that we are not
Mad. You see, before you came we were reviewing
The bitter consequences of this injustice on our
Family. Abod's wife left him one week ago.

Mola L.

Is that true, Abod?

Abod

As true as you are standing there.

Mola L.

What happened?

Lobe

Oh well, long story. The surface reason was that a
Dog bit one of their children and Abod took it out
On her.

Mola L.

I fail to see the connection between a dog biting a
Child and Abod taking it out on his wife.

Abod

That's precisely where the problem is. We believe
That the bite was merely a spark applied to the
Gunpowder barrel of poverty, embezzlement,
Handcuffs, (*with rising frenzy*) communication
Monopoly, dungeons, arrests, censorship, toll
Gates, capital flight, windscreen licenses, Ghandis,
Coups de coeurs, of the miasma of
Tribalism, nepotism, regionalism, segregation,
Deforestation, devaluation, hoarding, kicks, slaps,
Summary executions, civil disobedience,
Democratic distortions; (*calmly*) the barrel of the
Ultimate realization that we are born at the wrong
Time, in the wrong place.

Mola L.

You now begin to understand why I cannot
Function in this kind of environment. I am all cut
Out for a society that upholds the mystique of talent
And the invigorating power of justice.

Yeza

La justice, le talent, c'est bien d'en parler, mais
Hélas pas sous les tropiques. Ces deux principes
Constituent à eux seuls le socle de toute civilisation.
L'occident ne le sait que trop. Mais passons.
Il s'agit pour nous maintenant de voir comment
Récupérer notre chère épouse.

Lobe

Poignant are your words. Talent and justice
Are the bedrock of any civilization. But we must
Also not lose sight of the fact that survival,
Collective survival, is the driving force of all
Civilization. How ready are for the fight?
How committed are we to
The pursuit of the collective good? Me first, me last.
After me the deluge. You cannot implant justice and

Talent on barren soil. These cardinal principles take
Root and blossom when they are placed at the service
Of man. They wither and die when held
In criminal bondage by the greed of men.

Mola L.

We've got an urgent problem on our hands.
Has anyone been to see our wife since she went
Away?

Abod

None of us has, but people have come to tell me she
Says I am possessed and that on no account will she
Return to my house. I understand she has even flung
Her wedding ring into the bush.

Lobe

Well, don't bother about what she might or might not
Have done with her wedding ring. Those might just be
The words of an aggrieved woman. This bit about your
Being possessed ought to be investigated, I think.

Abod

Investigated? What do you mean?

Lobe

African metaphysics, forgotten? You may not believe
In their powers, but let me tell you those powers exist.

Yeza

Si, si, Monsieur!

Lobe

Consult a diviner and let us know his findings.
They might provide a good angle from which to tackle
The problem.

Abod

Me. In a diviner's temple. Magic in Jerusalem!

Curtain

Scene 8

Abod alone on stage

Abod

Me, in a diviner's. Real magic in Jerusalem. Diviners.
Fakes, all of them. If they could see the invisible,
Divine the future, they would long since have cured
Africa of its myriad ills. No! I will not allow myself to
Be abused in broad daylight. I will be my own diviner.
Now I remember! Bi used to complain of sexual
Harassment. I know the idiot. The ugly fool. The
Thoroughly detestable son of a ganakoh! *(Kneels and takes out*
cowries from his pocket. Throws them on the floor and examines them like
a diviner) Ah! Now! There it is. Abod, your house is
Not well. You said a dog surged from nowhere and
Bit your daughter. It's all clearly stated out here
Before me. I can see it. Even the blind can see it. The
Bite was no ordinary bite. The dog came to deliver a
Message. I see a man. An idiot. An ugly fool. I see him
Covering a beautiful woman with lecherous looks.
(Collects the cowries and throws them again, studies them, and then breaks
out in derisive laughter) The thoroughly detestable son of a
Ganakoh. What did he think? Here it is before me: the
Beautiful woman will not, I repeat <u>not</u> have any of his
Dirty games. Ah! My faithful wife. *(Rising)* But Abod,
Remember she said you were possessed. How do you
Resolve that? Let's see. Simple. We will have it on
Record, on my record, that he consulted a soothsayer
Who told him that so long as my wife was in my house
She would be faithful, unbendingly and unbendably
Faithful. So they brought the dog to chase her out. But
He will be disillusioned soon enough. My wife is gone
Physically, but emotionally, sentimentally, she is with
Me, here, in my heart.
(Clutches his heart).

Curtain.

Scene 9

Near Tita's house

Tita

(*Visibly angry*)

What is this world coming to? You send my
Daughter away from your house and sit there
Comfortably for two weeks. As if that is not enough
Insult, the day you care to show up you stand by the
Roadside and order me there. God forbid. Did I make
A mistake by giving you my daughter free? How can
You push ingratitude to such a point?

Abod

Father, I am deeply sorry for what has happened.
I understand your anger, but please let me explain a
Few things to you.

Tita

You had better, and fast too.

Abod

You certainly misunderstood the reason for my not
Wanting to enter the house this morning.

Tita

And what were they?

Abod

Bi says I am possessed!

Tita

And I confirm you are, by the looks of it. She says you
Behave like a beast. That when the evil spirit seizes
You a thick smell of death descends on the house.
You become wild, bestial. You are not out to correct
But to kill. You torture her and glory in her agony.
(*More sternly*) That's the only daughter I have. If so much as a
Strand of hair ever gets missing from her head, then
You will see me as you have never seen me before.

Abod

I hope such a day never comes. That's why I went to
Find out just what this talk of my being possessed was

31

All about. My friends Yeza and Lobe advised that I
Consult a diviner. They even recommended one for
Me, down at mile three-six.

Tita

Leke Umbi.

Abod

Yes, that's the name.

Tita

Aha! I know them all. There's another one at
Bonakanda, but that one is for people who have
Nothing to do with their money. You went to the
Right place. Leke Umbi is good. You remember
When your mother-in-law started giving me trouble
Because I wanted to marry Kah Tema. It was Leke
Umbi who worked on her. He did such a good job
That she actually went and brought me Kah Tema
Herself. (*He's been nodding his acquiescence all along*)
Leke Umbi is next only to God in his divining
Powers.

Abod

As soon as I entered his temple he looked at
Me and shook his head and said my house was not well. That was
The first thing that impressed me. Just how this man
Knew that my house was not well I could not tell.

Tita

Ah! He knows. He knows it all.

Abod

I told him about the dog incident and the whole
Secret unfolded before him. As he cast his cowries
He was like entranced, illuminated (*Mimicking diviner*)
He throws the cowries, questions them, searches
My look, returns to the cowries, flips his hand at
Me, then points to the truth lying there before him
On the floor. Ah! Now! There it is, Abod. Your
House is not well. You said a dog surged from
Nowhere and bit your daughter. Here it is!
Here, before me. I can see it. Even the blind can
See it. That bite was no ordinary bite.

Tita

Hee? No ordinary bite? So Leke Umbi saw it.
Even me I saw it. I knew that that bite was no
Ordinary bite.

Abod

No! That bite was no ordinary bite. Leke Umbi's
Face is glowing. He has the truth in his hand. His
Cowries are sweating under the strain of the truth
They are about to yield. The dog came to deliver a
Message. I see a man. An idiot. An ugly fool. He
Is covering a beautiful woman with lecherous
Looks. Here Leke Umbi collects his cowries,
Throws them again, studies them attentively, and
Breaks into a big mocking laughter. The
Thoroughly detestable son of a ganakoh! What
Did he think? Here it is before me. The beautiful
Woman will not have any of his dirty games. So
Long as she is in her husband's house she will
Remain faithful, unbendingly and unbendably
Faithful.

Tita

(Nodding with pride)

Just like my daughter to be faithful,
Even onto death. Leke Umbi is a great diviner.
None of his words has ever been known to drop
To the ground.

Abod

That ugly idiot consulted another diviner who
Promised to get Bi out of my house. This, dear
Father, is how Bi came to leave the house. They
Sent the dog to quicken her departure. Leke Umbi
Warned me about it. He said my wife would
Leave the house vowing never to return, and my
Sight would become so offensive to her that
Each time she saw me she would reach for the
Nearest axe. He said to me: don't go near where
She is, not even to see your children. The only
Way they can succeed in keeping her away from

You is by making her hate you, and the more of
You she sees, the more she will hate you. That's
Why I could not enter the house this morning.

Tita

So that's the source of all this trouble. A man
Who wants to sleep with your wife.

Abod

If it was a man I wouldn't mind that much. But
We are talking about an idiot, an ugly fool, a
Thoroughly detestable son of a ganakoh!

Tita

Thank God you went to Leke Umbi. Now I see
The problem differently. You know we live in a
Vicious world. Men have overtaken women
In the power to spread evil and sorrow. A man
Must sleep with his friend's wife to feel himself
A man. Brother must sleep with sister, father
With daughter, mother with son. Ours is a world
Where everybody must sleep with everybody else.

Abod

Yes, father, we live in just one big, stinking
Sewage of fornication. Men's minds have
Become enchained by lust. Women are not
Human beings with dignity and a personality.
They are things to use, abuse and throw away.
In the night cars disappear into bushes and
Immediately tremble with the 40° fever of the
Flesh. In breezeless nights shrubs convulse as
If in the claws of a raging demon. It's a mad,
Mad world. Fathers are no longer fathers. They
Are lewd shapes stalking the innocent steps of anything
In skirts. The world has gone mad, crazy. We are receding
Into the savage darkness of our forefathers.

Tita

Abod, my son, I too had suspected that an evil force was
Controlling your home.

Abod

Indeed, father, and that is why I couldn't enter the house

This morning. She is at home, isn't she?

Tita

Yes, and swearing by all the gods that the marriage is over.

Abod

You see what I am saying?

Tita

Yes, but you must learn to fight those evil
Forces. You must not let them take control of
Your will. What you did to your wife was very
Bad. I've been married for thirty-two years
And I cannot remember having beaten my wife
More than twenty-eight times. And yet you
Know how mouthy and stubborn your
Mother-in-law is.

Abod

Like mother like daughter.

Tita

Not exactly because there is more of me in my
Daughter than her mother.

Abod

I was thinking of a Chinese proverb which says
That when the man sings and the wife
Accompanies there is harmony in the family,
But when the wife sings and the man
Accompanies the woman is holding the
Command baton. It's like a hen crowing.

Tita

God forbid! But what you did was wrong. If
You follow a woman's mouth you will kill her
And the mouth will still be talking. If a woman
Offends you, just keep quiet and watch her. If
You feel that you are getting angry, leave the
House. You know that all the woman's power is in
Her mouth, and the weaker she is the more
Poison her mouth will spit. I have seen men
Give their women one slap in anger and that
Slap has taken the women to their grave.

Abod

To repress a moment's anger may save you a
Hundred days of sorrow. Another Chinese
Proverb.

Tita

Well said. That should be your guiding principle
With women. Nothing a woman does or says
Should make you lose your calm to the point of
Exercising physical violence on her.

Abod

Women have long hair but short-sighted
Intelligence. Chinese proverb.

Tita

You seem to know the world of women very well,
So there is no reason why all this should be
Happening. Now let's think of what to do to make
Bi change her mind.

Abod

I will send a few trusted friends to talk to her.

Tita

(*Making for exit*)

But then make sure you are also present
Because at the end of the day it is a matter between
The two of you.

Curtain

Scene 10

In Tita's house.
(Bi is dumped at some corner. Tita moves over to her.)

Tita

Bi

Bi

(Absentmindedly)

Yes, Ba

Tita

How have you spent the day?

Bi

So so.

Tita

Did you go to work?

Bi

I wanted to, but I have such a heavy head!
I actually bathed and got dressed but I didn't find
The spirits to get out of the house.

Tita

It's wrong for you to stay locked up in the house all
The time. Go out and meet other people and talk to
Them. I don't say you discuss your problems with
The first person you meet. Talk about other things.
Discuss things that make you see life in a different
Light. When you listen to other people you will
Realize that you are not carrying the world on your
Head as you seem to think.

Bi

I understand, Ba. But I just do not feel like seeing
People now. I first of all want to get myself together
And see how to handle the new life that is opening up
Before me and the children.

Tita

Good thing you are thinking of your future and that
Of the children. I learnt one Chinese proverb today
Which I want you to reflect on seriously. The proverb

37

Says: repress a moment's anger and you will be
Spared a hundred days of sorrow. I think there's a lot
Of practical wisdom in that saying. (*With fatherly warmth*)
You see, anger is like a bomb. You never measure its
Damage until it has exploded. Very often it explodes
With such violence that it destroys beyond any hope
Of repair. And we who set it off are the first to regret.
We should learn at all times to sit on our anger and we
Will be the happier for it. (*Long pause, then affectionately*) Bi.

Bi

Ba.

Tita

I'm just from seeing your husband. He and I had a
Discussion which helped clear a few things in my
Head.

Bi

(*Angrily*)

Ba, I have told you and I still repeat,
I don't want to have anything to do with Abod
Anymore. So I hope you people discussed other
Things, not me.

Tita

We discussed your marriage, basically.

Bi

Ba, I have…

Tita

Why don't you just listen to me?

Bi

If it is about Abod you want to talk then you can
Be sure I will not listen.

Tita

It's precisely about him I want to talk and you will
Sit here and listen.

Bi

I will sit here, but know you are talking to a stone.

Tita

Not if there's a jot of my blood in your veins. You
Don't solve a problem by running away from it. If

This matter concerned only you and your husband,
I would not worry my tired limbs over it. My
Grandchildren, it's they I am worried about.

Bi

Ba, if you have those children's interest at heart then
You should help hasten my divorce. I have already
Found a house, I told you, and I am now looking for
A van to pick up what is still left of my things in
Abod's house. I think that's where you can help me
And the children.

Tita

(*Laughing softly*)

When I hear you talk you remind me very
Much of your mother when she was your age. I can't
Count the number of times she packed you and your
Brothers out of the house; at times just because a
Thought crossed her mind that I had the intention of
Considering the possibility of feeling like wanting to
Look at another woman.

Bi

If my mother does not know how to take decisions
And stick to them, that's her cup of tea. The two of
You know the game you were playing. Right now I
Am not in for any game. My children and I are going
And that's the end of the matter. I can't stand the
Sight of that brute anymore.

Tita

I don't know much about his being a brute, but what
I know for certain is that he is a charming young man
Who loves you and the children immensely. Why
Don't you see that side of him too? Think of the
Father and the husband in your man.

Bi

Father and husband indeed. Abod is a monster! Curse
Be the day our paths met. (*In near hysteria*). I hate
Him, Ba, you can never imagine how much I hat Abod.
(*Breaks down*).

39

Tita

(In mock regret)

I'm sorry, my daughter. I didn't know that the
Harm was so deep. I thought there was still some
Way to mend the situation. You see, what I am
Doing I am doing in the interest of the children and
You. Several times I have seen you and your
Husband in perfect union and communion and I
Have thanked God for your family. Every word
Of your last letter to me continues to ring in my
Head. (*Reading from offstage as both listen attentively*).

    Ba,

    Abod flew off to London yesterday. The children
    And I were at the airport to see him off. When his
    Flight was called we all hugged one another and our
    Tears mingled. My husband has been gone for only
    One day but already I feel so lonely. Ba, don't be
    Worried about me. It's a soft, happy kind of
    Loneliness. I sleep in Abod's pyjamas. That way his
    Absence is so much easier to bear. The children too
    Miss him very much. He is such a rallying force in
    The home. I feel so empty and helpless when he is
    Not there. (*pacing away from him*).

This was your last letter to me, so I thought we could yet
Repair things, but now I see we can't. Divorce is the
Only course left. (*Bi cringes but her father who is not looking at her fails
to see it*). Since you say you already have a
House things will move even faster. (*Bi puts out her hand but drops it
again when her father fails to pick up the signal*).
I will start by obtaining separation, first thing
Tomorrow. (*Bi coughs uneasily*). The minute that
Is done, I will set the divorce proceeding in motion.
I'm sure the courts have some way of expediting
Divorce suits like this one where there is a clear
Case for it. How silly of me to have wanted to
Mend the irreparable. (*Facing her*). Where did you
Say your new house was?

Bi
(*Somewhat confusedly*)
I saw one in Bomaka and another one
In Bokwai.

Tita
You don't intend to park into both houses, do you?

Bi
No Ba, no. Only, I'm worried about the state of both
Houses. The one in Bokwai has no water facilities
And is lost in a thick bush. The one in Bomaka is in
A very rowdy area and I understand it's a hideout for
Thieves.
(*Enter Lobe and Yeza*).

Yeza
(*Exuberantly*)
Ma chérie! Mais ça fait toute une éternité !
Tu nous as beaucoup manqué tu sais.

Tita
How is Monsieur le Professeur?

Yeza
Je me porte assez bien, mais je me porterai encore
Mieux quand notre épouse sera de nouveau avec
Nous.

Bi
Tu veux que je parler français ? Je suis quitter ton
Frère.
(*Breaks into laughter*).

Lobe
I didn't know your French was so good.

Yeza
Non! Non! Son français est tout simplement
Merveilleux. Your French is veri veri gut!

Bi
Thank you.

Lobe
After all these civilities, can we now talk business?

Yeza
Tout à fait!

Lobe

Bi, one day two weeks ago you woke me up early
In the morning. The state you were in froze the
Blood in my veins. I don't want to recall all those
Moments. Thy are so painful. Since then I have
Not had the courage to come here because I
Wouldn't have known what to say once I got here.
But I have followed your words and deeds. In
Particular, I have admired the irrevocable
Determination with which you have said no! to all
Entreaties on Abod's behalf.

Tita

I am not cutting you short, but before you came I
Was praising her for her firmness. It is good for a
Woman to take a decision and stick to it.

Lobe

Especially when such a decision is founded on
Reasons that defy all challenge.

Yeza

(*Cutting in noisily*)

Je peux aussi dire quelque chose non!
Alors ! Voyez-vous, j'ai toujours eu pour cette
Dame beaucoup d'admiration. Depuis que je la
Connais, je n'ai jamais rien eu à lui reprocher.
Voilà pourquoi j'ai pris très au sérieux sa décision
De quitter ce Monsieur. Si elle en est arrivée là,
Cela voudrait dire qu'elle a bien mûri sa décision.

Lobe

Yes. This woman put everything she had into this
Marriage: her love, her passion, her sweat, her
Tears. She gave up family and friends, wealth and
Leisure, so that nothing, nobody, could steal a
Pinch of her attention. Abod took her commitment
For granted. Her love was a right, her faithfulness
A free gift. She deserved nothing in return, not
Even a faint sign of appreciation. (*Bi tries to intervene*).
No! save your breath. I know how you feel. I am
Here to articulate your indignation, to give lasting

Form to your resolve. One word only I know that
Will put Abod in his place: divorce. One word only
I can summon up that will educate him conclusively
In the art of manhood: divorce. Mrs Abod, Yeza
And I have come to bring you our total support for
The just and rightful decision you have taken to
Divorce Abod.

Bi

Can I …

Yeza

Ne parlez point, Madame. Rien qu'à vous voir on
Comprend tout, tout de suite. Vous êtes excédée
Par les agissements de cet homme, et vous êtes
Maintenant décidée, plus que jamais, à en finir une
Bonne fois pour toutes. Et c'est très bien ainsi.
Ça lui apprendra à jouer avec son mariage !

Bi

All what you have said…

Tita

My dear friends, you have expressed my thoughts
More clearly than I could have done.

Bi
(Frantically)

Ba!

Tita

Yes, daughter, we have to act fast in your interest
And that of the children. While I am in court
Tomorrow obtaining separation, Lobe and Yeza
Will get a van and clear the rest of your things
From that man's house. And he will be well
Advised not to obstruct them.

Yeza

Oui! Oui! Qu'il essaie ! Il n'ignore pas que je
Suis ceinture noire, cinquième dan.
(Whips the air with a few karate strokes)

Lobe

Besides, we will hire the services of three policemen.

43

Bi

(*Visibly worried*)

Do you mean...

Lobe

Oh yes! If Abod tries anything funny tomorrow
He will see me at my funniest too. You know
That our police do not ask questions. They act.
And they are the swifter in action the more beers
You promise them. Don't be surprised tomorrow
To hear that a stray bullet from a well focused
Revolver shattered his skull. (*Bi screams hysterically. Enter Abod*).

Bi

(*Rushing to his embrace*)

Abod, my husband! How relieved
I am to see you! I was afraid you wouldn't come
And tomorrow a stray bullet from a well focused
Revolver would shatter your skull.

Abod

(*Feigning surprise*)

A stray bullet? Shatter my skull? And
Where was the stray bullet going to come from?

Bi

(*Pointing somewhat accusedly at the other three*).

That's what
They said. They were going to bring the police
To our home (*the others exchange looks of victory*) tomorrow
And if you tried anything funny one of those
Police guns was going to empty its load in your head.
They wanted to come and clear my things from
Our home. I do not know when I asked them to
Come and help me. They have been pressurizing
Me, refusing me the right to even say a word.

Lobe and Tita

Suicide! Suicide! And when you are shown the
Noose you scream for life!

Yeza

Mais au fond, ces deux-là, de qui se moquent-ils?
(*All four stick up their thumbs in victory*).   *Curtain. End.*

44

Things Fall in Place

(Inspired by

Things Fall Apart)

Characters

Okonkwo, Hardworking villager
Nnadi, His friend. Later Peter
Ezeugo, villagers
Nwoye, Okonkwo's son
Ikemefuna, Captive son
Virgin girl
Ebeka and Ekwefi, Okonkwo's wives
Elders of Umuofia
White Priest
Interpreter
African converts
District Commissioner
Jonas Okereke
James, Messengers to the Commissioner
Osu, village outcasts

Scene 1

Market square

(Villagers in expectant mood. Festival music fills the air. Bare-chested young men flex muscles to the excited applause of young girls. Enter Okonkwo and Amalinze the cat from opposing ends, each showing off his wrestling skills. Crowd cheers them on. They wrestle and Okonkwo throws the cat after a well-matched fight. Villagers sweep Okonkwo off amidst shouts of victory. Sudden hush as Nnadi storms in.)

Nnadi
(Harshly)
Down! Set him down!

Villagers
(Confusedly)
What? Why? Has he not won? We celebrate his victory.

Okonkwo
(To villagers)
On with the victory song! Amalinze can drink
the running water of his grandfather if he wants!
(Villagers surround him and dance to the victory song)

Nnadi
(More harshly)
Stop! I say stop! What do you celebrate?

Okonkwo
(Stepping forward resolutely)
Nnadi, what is in all this?
Why do you want to spoil my victory? Did I give that
weakling dust to eat? Or did I not?

1ˢᵗ villager
That throw. Was it not the victory throw?

2ⁿᵈ villager
Who has ever recovered from such a throw?

Okonkwo
If I did not win, where is Amalinze? Shame has shut his
mouth and driven him into hiding. Nnadi, your jealousy will
not spoil this festival. *(To villagers)* Let us dance! *(Dance resumes)*

Nnadi

Ha! ha! ha! He calls me jealous. *(Pushing villagers sternly behind him and talking into Okonkwo's face)* Okonkwo, son of Unoka, many years ago before your mother's womb spat you to this earth, Ojiafor threw Agbrada...in this very place.
Each year after that, a man threw another man. Then came the year Chinedu demolished Okeke... here ...in this very field.
Just last year, you know it, even the sun stopped its journey to watch Ezebuzor, lion man of Oniaburo,
and Chike the tiger. Then it went on its journey. *(Solemnly)* Okonkwo, son of Unoka, the sun does not rise and remain in one place: it journeys. And your mind must journey with it.
If your mind stays in one place it will see sun where there is but moon, morning when the old snore . *(With grave insistence)* Your mind must travel with the sun. What you celebrate as victory may be but a death cry. Dance well, but know that for which you dance. *(Makes for exit, then stops)* Change this victory dance. News is here at our doorsteps of men without colour.

2nd villager

Men without colour.... Ghosts ha! ha! ha!...they are ghosts!

Nnadi

Call them what you like, but they are here.

Okonkwo

No ghost can stand me. I have strength enough to throw five of them in any wrestling match.

Nnadi

These ones we talk about are not Amalinze or Uchendu or Nnamibie. They are wrestlers of another kind.

Okonkwo

(With assertive pride)

I am here waiting for them. The
ghost who can throw me in a wrestling match is not yet born. *(Laughs heartily)* Let them count the cracks on Amalinze's ribs. *(Etches a wrestling swoop to rousing applause)*

Curtain

49

Scene 2

Marketplace
Crowded and hushed. Low voices are heard here and there, but the faces are grim. Ogbuefi Nnadi rises.

Nnadi
Umuofia kwenu!

Villagers
Yaa!

Nnadi
Kwenu!

Villagers
Yaa!

Nnadi
Kwenu!

Villagers
Yaa!

Nnadi
(Pointing in the direction of Mbaino)
Those uncircumcised
animals have killed a daughter of Umuofia. *(Bows his head and gnashes his teeth as a murmur of suppressed anger sweeps through the crowd)* Mbeke the wife of Ogbuefi Udo is
no more. *(With vigorous anger)* Umuofia kwenu!

Villagers
Yaa!

Nnadi
Kwenu!

Villagers
Yaa!

Nnadi
We want reparation. *(Murmurs of approval from crowd)* Mbaino has killed our daughter. You don't dare a tiger and get away with it. Or do you? *(Nods of disapproval from crowd)*. You sent me to Okonkwo and I went. And I delivered the message as you gave it to me. He left for Mbaino early this morning to bring us back their…*(Enter Okonkwo with a boy and a girl)* Ah! There he comes!

50

(Excited noises greet Okonkwo's return) Elders of Umuofia, hold your tongues. We sent a son of this village on an errand. Let us hear how he travelled. You don't taste pepper by only looking at it. Let us hear the words that Okonkwo will say to us.

Okonkwo

Elders of Umuofia I greet you. I have come back from where you sent me. I have come back proud to be a son of Umuofia. Mbaino received me as a tethered goat would receive a wronged lion. They knew they had done a wrong thing to Umuofia.

Elder

A bad thing indeed!

Okonkwo

As you elders say, when a child leaves the house, it might bring you a panload of trouble. The elders of Mbaino blamed the murder of Ogbuefi Udo's wife on their young men. But does a father give up a son because he has done wrong?

Elders

No!

Okonkwo

Mbaino accepted blame for the killing of our daughter and sent this young lad and this virgin to appease the wrath of Umuofia.

(Elders examine the two children closely and nod their approval)

Nnadi

Thank you Okonkwo. What you have done is good. This is how a man should talk. We sent Okonkwo to Mbaino because we knew he had a man's voice in his chest.
It is good for a village to have a son with muscles and a strong voice. *(Elders nod their approval)* Elders of Umuofia! I speak with your mouths, or don't I?

Elders

Ugbuefi Nnadi you have our mouth!

Nnadi

I thank you. We know how it goes. Ugbuefi Udo shall have the maiden from Mbaino. He who breaks a tapper's calabash must place a new one before him. A man is no

man without a woman. Ugbuefi Udo shall have the maiden
as wife. He must wield his machete once again with
steaming pounded yam in his belly. *(With attractive
emphasis)* In the night he must eat bearded meat.

Elders
(In confused voices)

Yea! Yea!

1ˢᵗ elder

And good bearded meat too.

2ⁿᵈ elder

Soft and ripe, like the pear that goes with roasted cassava.

Nnadi

Wipe your mouths! This matter is not all food and bed. We
have given back to Ugbuefi Udo that which was his. As for
the boy Ikemefuna, Okonkwo shall have full custody over
him. *(Turning to Okonkwo)* Here! Take him home and
produce him whenever Umuofia so demands.
*(Okonkwo receives frightened child. Exit all except Nnadi, Okonkwo and
Ikemefuna).*

Okonkwo

Nnadi! I'm worried. Night is overtaking us. Mbaino have
lost their manly ways. They now behave like women. When
they greet you their voice is weak, like that of a woman.
Many of them no longer wear our loincloths. They have
cut holes in cloth, like mad men. I even saw women
carrying twin children. Chineke forbid! I wanted to seize
them and fling them into Miniwekwu.

Nnadi
(Laughing)

They would sooner have flung *you* into the river!

Okonkwo
(Spiritedly)

Me! In the place of twins!

Nnadi

You will not understand until you are ready for the new fight.
Mbaino are already winning theirs. We used to say Umuofia
was the handsome young man of our clan. But I don't
know whether we can still say that.

Okonkwo

Why not? You say handsome. Where have you left our strength?
We are handsome and strong. (*Then solemnly*)
Ogbuefi Nnadi, I need your help. Perhaps you can already
guess what it is. I have cleared a farm but have no yams to
sow. I know what it is to ask a man to trust another with
yams, especially these days when young men are afraid of
hard work. I am not afraid of hard work. The lizard that
jumped from the high iroko tree to the ground said he would
praise himself if nobody else did. I began to fend for myself
at an age when most people still suck at their mother's
breasts. If you give me some yam seeds I shall not fail you.

Nnadi

(*Clearing his throat*) It pleases me to see a young man like you
these days when our youth have gone soft. Many young men
have come to me to ask for yams but I have refused because I
knew they would just dump them in the earth and leave them
to be choked by weeds. When I say no to them they think I am
hard-hearted. But it is not so. Eneke the bird says that since
men have learnt to shoot without missing, he has learnt to fly
without perching. I have learnt to be stingy with my yams. But
I can trust you. As our fathers said, you can tell a ripe corn
by its looks. I shall give you twice four hundred yams. Go
ahead and prepare your farm.

Okonkwo

(*Making his exit*)
The ancestors will bless you. And all the gods.

Nnadi

Brave young man. Yes. Only he says he can wrestle with
the newcomers without colour. May Amadioha keep him
from it! Ezebufor slapped one of them in Mbaino and was
found the following day with small small stones in his body,
and flies in his torn mouth. That is what awaits any man who
wrestles with the newcomer without colour: small small stones in
the body, and flies in a torn mouth.

Curtain

Scene 3

In Okonkwo's compound

(Makes triumphant entry with Ikemefuna carrying his bag, to ululations from wives.)

Okonkwo
(With show of muscular strength)

What do they call him?

Ebeka
(Circling round husband in praise songs)

Amalinze.

Ekwefi
(Mockingly)

Amalinze. *(Hands akimbo)* Could he?

Ebeka

Where? Obanje man.

Okonkwo

You have said it, my wife. Obanje…beast without penis!
(Wives laugh excitedly) He came to fight me a second
time. Me, Okonkwo. Man of many wives.

Ebeka

Whose yams feed Umuofia and even Mbaino!

Ekwefi

Whose obi Amadioha himself built!

Ebeka

Man without compare! Taker of titles!

Ekwefi

Who stings, like a cobra!

Okonkwo
(To Ekwefi)

I should have sent you to throw him.
(Ululation by both wives) He was never my match! *(To Ebeka)*
You heard Nnadi again. *(Sits down)* Like the first time, this my
second victory turned his stomach. He wanted to stop the victory
dance.

Ekwefi

Idemili forbid! My Lord, like the first time, I heard him talk about some strange kind of men again.

Okonkwo

Men without colour.

Ebeka

Yes. But why is he always talking about them?

Okonkwo

The job of idle heads.

Ekwefi

But we have such people here, and we throw them in the Evil Forest!

Okonkwo

He says these his own are good wrestlers.

Ekwefi

(Derisive laughter)

They will be for me. Let them come.

(Loosens and reties cloth in mock combat readiness).

Okonkwo

(Reflecting proudly)

Men without colour. If the gods have denied them even colour, then what are they? I will lift them by the ear and feed them to my pigs. No! The pigs will run away.

I will lift them like dry wood…bear them on my shoulders, and carry them to Evil Forest. I will offer them in sacrifice to Amadioha. Ha! ha! ha! A banquet! Banquet of the gods! Idemili! Miniwekwu! And all the gods of Umuofia! They will feed on the flesh and bones of the men without colour. Evil Forest will swell, grow more evil still with their uneaten remains. For the gods choose their meal. *(Calling to backstage)* Nwoye! *(No response. Stolen exit by Ekwefi)* Nwoye-e-e-e! *(No response)*

Ebeka

Do you want something, my lord?

Okonkwo

But where is that cold ash? Some of these new diseases come and only pick you in the heart. I'll burst his stomach. *(To Ikemefuna softly)* Ike, the calabash by my bedside…get it. I need to drink in readiness. As I celebrate the victories of today, I must prepare for the battles of tomorrow. *(Exit Ikemefuna. Enter Nwoye)* You this thing! *(Nwoye starts backwards)* I called a long time ago. *(Enter*

55

Ikemefuna with calabash and horn. Pours Okonkwo a hornful. He gulps it down and hands horn back to Ikemefuna who stands by his side ready to pour some more. Turning to Nwoye who has stood transfixed at some distance all this while) I called and you refused to come.

Nwoye

I did not hear.

Okonkwo

(*Rising and edging towards him*) Eh eh? (*Wife moves to one corner in apprehension. Nwoye steps backwards towards exit*) Were you in this house?

Nwoye

No.

Okonkwo
(*Edging ever closer*)

At the wrestling field then?

Nwoye

No.

Okonkwo
(*With mounting rage*)

No eh? So you did not watch me throw
Amalinze. *(To audience)* Lift him like gbodimi leaf, and
throw on the ground.*(Then back at Nwoye)* How then can
you fight if you do not see me fight? How can you win if you
do not see me win? All Umuofia was at the wrestling field
to hail me. But you were not there. Are you not a son of this
village? *(Silence. Roaring.)* Speak! Are you my son or not? Are
you of this village or not? (*Raises hand to strike son. Ebeka
closes eyes in fright. Enter Nnadi panting*).

Nnadi

Stop! These are wrong enemies. The ones you should fight
are yet to come. Cutting down a home stem is a job anyone can
do. The forest of the unknown and its millennial iroko, that's
where you show you are a man.

Okonkwo

But have I not done that? Is there any greater victory, any sweeter
triumph than to put your foot on the head of your rival? I put my
foot on Amalinze's head.

Nnadi

That victory belongs to its own time. But a bigger fight
awaits you ahead. You only bark at your son. If you continue
like this, you will soon be alone: no sons, no wives.

Okonkwo

I prefer to be alone than have cold ash for a son. I will
tear open his stomach and remove the bad spirit in it.
Unless I did not deliver him. (*Harshly to Nwoye*) Out of my sight!
(*Nwoye rushes out to looks of consternation from Ebeka and Nnadi. Exit
Nnadi*)

Okonkwo
(*At Ebeka*)

Where is Ekwefi?

Ebeka

She has gone to plait her hair.

Okonkwo

And her children, did she take them?

Ebeka

They are here.

Okonkwo

Did she ask you to feed them before she went?

Ebeka

Yes.
(*Ekwefi sidles in*)

Okonkwo
(*Sternly*)

Where are you from? (*Pounces on frightened woman*)

Ekwefi

Help! oh! help! I'm dead.
(*Ebeka pleads from a helpless distance*)

Okonkwo
(*Still fuming*)

Ike!

Ikemefuna

Father!

Okonkwo

My gun!... from my obi!...quick! (*Ebeka throws hands about with fright*)

Ekwefi

(In an audible murmur)

Gun indeed! A gun that never shoots.

Okonkwo

Heh? Did I hear well? What did she say? My gun? Not shoot? *(Enter Ikemefuna with gun. Okonkwo seizes it and aims at Ekwefi as she takes flight. Fires amidst wailing by Ebeka. Ekwefi collapses more out of fright than harm. Okonkwo examines her and storms out. Ekwefi rises and sticks out her tongue in his direction. Women fill the air with laughter)*

Ebeka

Ekwe, this your mouth!

Ekwefi

(Coyly)

Ah! Nne! Leave me. Oko worries me too much.

Ebeka

You are his die. Who doesn't know it? I had my turn. Now is yours. *(Drum from offstage)*

Ekwefi

(With visible excitement)

Nne, who would not like a man like Oko? I will not lie to you. I like him. See that wrestling match. He swept Amalinze off his feet and held him high up in the air like a banana leaf. Tears came to my eyes

and my heart said *that* was him, *that* was my man. When he beats me I see that day and his strokes become like palm-oil on my body.

Ebeka

(With some jealousy)

Then why did you marry Nzekwu?

Ekwefi

(Shrugging)

Hmm!…marry…you call that marriage? My beauty turned Nzekwu's head. *(Ebeka casts a half-admiration, half-jealousy look at her)* He blinded my father with cowries and expensive cloth, so in the end I said let me obey my parents. I knew I was not going to stay in Nzekwu's house

for more than one week. I never allowed him to touch me, not even once. I had vowed that Okonkwo would be my man, so I saved all of this *(showing off her beauty)* for him.
(Enter Nnadi)

Nnadi
I greet this house.

Ebeka
Ogbuefi Nnadi, come softly.

Nnadi
Thank you. And your man Okonkwo, where is he?

Ebeka
He just went out. We will send for him. Ogbuefi, have a seat. Ike!

Ikemefuna
(From backstage)
Nne! *(Comes running in).*

Ebeka
Go for your father. He must be in Obiaka's compound. Tell him Ogbuefi Nnadi is here.
(Exit Ikemefuna)

Nnadi
Ekwefi, my young girl, you look well-fed.

Ekwefi
Thank you, Ogbuefi. I am happy in my marriage.

Nnadi
That is good. Your man is very fond of you. I know that.

Ekwefi
Only his hand, Ogbuefi. His hand is too sharp! If he is talking to you, you must only stand at a distance. Even so... chei!

Nnadi
(Laughing)
That's just him. But he should not raise his hand on you again. I will tell him. *(Throwing knowing look at Ekwefi)* Has your throat started giving you trouble?

Ekwefi
(Perplexed)
A lot, Ogbuefi. I always feel like eating
calabar chalk.

Nnadi

That's good. I will tell your man. He must not raise his hand on you again or even shout at you... before many moons.

Ekwefi

Will he even listen? He nearly killed me a few moments ago because I went to look for calabar chalk.

Nnadi

Leave that to me.
(*Enter Okonkwo and Ikemefuna*)

Okonkwo

Ogbuefi Nnadi, come well (*To the wives*) Leave us alone. (*Exit wives*) Ogbuefi, our eyes have not met for some days.

Nnadi

That is true. The things to do are many. Each time
I get up to come here, something else happens. It is always good to visit from time to time. That way any new seed that sprouts you will see. I have seen Ekwefi and I'm glad. But she has reported you to me.

Okonkwo

You mind that stubborn girl?

Nnadi

(*Paternally*)
You have done good work. Don't spoil it with your harsh ways. All she needs now is care. But that's not why I have come. (*To Ikemefuna*) Ike! go and help your mothers. (*Exit Ikemefuna. To Okonkwo solemnly*) Oko!

Okonkwo

Hmm!

Nnadi

I have come to talk to you about this child. What does he call you?

Okonkwo

Why? He calls me father of course.

Nnadi

I am glad to hear you say so. He calls you father. You know what that means. Do not bear a hand in his death.

Okonkwo

Eh?

Nnadi

Yes, just as I say. Umuofia has decided to kill him. The Oracle of the Hills and the Caves has pronounced it. They will take him outside the village as is the custom and kill him there. Do not have anything to do with it. He calls you
Father.

Okonkwo

You are telling me to disobey the gods ! Nnadi, that's a heavy thing to put on my head.

Nnadi

Okonkwo my friend, the gods are not in this. Beware of wrestling matches you cannot win. The world is no longer in the hands of the gods.

Okonkwo

(Rising in roaring laughter to a spirited performance)
Amadioha! Idemili! Mini Weku! Hear this! Your shrines are rabble! Empty, your groves! Your river power gone! The world has left you and journeyed to the men without colour! *(To Nnadi)* How can your mind be so feeble? The gods are strong.
Stronger now than ever. You breathe their will, you eat their will. The Oracle has spoken their will! And it will be done! The ransom child will die! And if it is my hand to do the will of the gods, then so be it! I will cut him down as the gods demand!
(Ritual gongs offstage)

Nnadi

Okonkwo, your stubbornness is leading you
the wrong way.

Okonkwo

My people's ways, that's all I live for!

Nnadi

Those ways are changing, my friend.

Okonkwo

I see no changes. Only the gods whose will
must be done! *(Storming out)* And it *will* be done! *(Exit)*

Nnadi

(Calling after him desperately)

Oko!…Oko! Stay! *(Crestfallen)* A river that wanders alone surely misses its course. The chick that spites its mother is sure food for hawks. How else can I make him see reason? Times have changed. The men without colour are here. Mbaino have welcomed them and saved their own head from death. We cannot see the gathering storm and continue to play outside like careless children.

Curtain

Scene 4

In Okonkwo's house
(He is sitting alone, brooding. Machete in sheath lies down his side.)

Okonkwo
(Listlessly)
Ike! Ike-e-e!

Ike
(From backstage)
Father! *(Comes rushing in)*

Okonkwo
(Languidly)
Sit down. Take that stool and sit down….here…by me. *(Ikemefuna sits down by him)* That's good.
(Places warm hand on Ikemefuna's back and looks at him affectionately for a while. Ikemefuna also returns loving looks. Okonkwo tries to speak but fails. Removes kola nut from bag and chews noisily. Then looking away). Ike…

Ike
Father!

Okonkwo
The wrestling match.

Ike
Yes Father. The one of two days ago.

Okonkwo
Yes. Did you see it?

Ike
Father, who in Umuofia did not? I saw it.

Okonkwo
And you liked it?

Ike
Father, I was proud. Happy.

Okonkwo
It pleases me to hear that.

Ike
(Looking at him in the eyes).
Father, I want to tell you something.

Okonkwo

Yes.

Ike

I'm proud of you. I want to be like you when I become a man.

Okonkwo

May that day come, my son.

Ike

Father, in seven, eight years I will take a wife. I will look for a wife like mama Ebeka.

Okonkwo

May the gods hear your words, my son.

Ike

My yamfield will cover many valleys, like yours. I will work day and night, like you.

Okonkwo

May it all come to pass, my son.

Iked

(Ever more excitedly)

Father, tell me, will I return to Mbaino?

Okonkwo

(Startled)

Mbaino? That's for the elders to decide. *(Silence)* Ike!

Ike

(Looking into his eyes anxiously)

Yes father.

Okonkwo

Tomorrow... *(Silence)*

Ike

Tomorrow.

Okonkwo

Ouf! Never mind.

Ike

As you please, father.

Okonkwo

It will come.

Ike

What, father?

Okonkwo

Tomorrow.

Ike

Tomorrow will surely come. And after tomorrow too.

Okonkwo

Tomorrow. Not after tomorrow. Only tomorrow matters.
Not after tomorrow. (*Visible signs of nervousness*)
It's tomorrow I talk about.

Ike

Father, you are sweating.

Okonkwo

(*Wiping his forehead*)
Me? No. Oh yes. Ah! Never mind.
Go. Your wrestling session. It's today. Don't stay away
from it.

Ike

I can go tomorrow, father.

Okonkwo

(*Growing irritated*)
Today. Go today. Tomorrow? *(Exit Ike)*
Tomorrow…tomorrow… not for you. The gods have willed it
so. There will be no tomorrow for you. Even as I speak I see it.
Wrestle today. The gods await your spirit tomorrow. One stroke
only. Not two. (*Moving towards exit*) Ransom children never suffer
two strokes. Only one. *(Owl hooting offstage. Listens.)* Too late. They
are here.

*(Enter grim-faced elders clad in black, lips sealed with grass blades. Ikemefuna
is in their midst, a pot of palmwine on his head. They stand the lad in the
centre and perform a cult dance round him. Suddenly one of them strikes the
pot on the boy's head. As pot shatters to the ground, boy turns to Okonkwo
shouting 'Father! They have killed me!' Okonkwo cuts him down. Elders
dance round the corpse, clanging their machetes, then file out, Okonkwo with
them, leaving body alone onstage. Enter Nnadi)*

Nnadi

(In a mixture of protest and supplication)

Ani! This is your
work. Violent death! Innocence murdered! Land defiled! Your
name wronged! Tomorrow, yes, tomorrow Okonkwo and his
family must flee to his motherland. And we your messengers
will come down with punishment on whatever he leaves behind.
We shall set fire to his houses, demolish his red walls, kill his
animals, destroy his barns. *(Pause, then dolefully)* A life-time of
hard work shall turn to dust. *(Crying out)*. Ani! And you the gods
of Umuofia, I ask you: this child lying here, tell me his crime.
Was he wrong to cry out *Father* to the man who fed him? And my
own twin children I threw away, what crime did they commit?
What crime, those children, hardly born? *(Softly)*. What crime?
(Goes down on his knees over the body)

Curtain

Scene 5

Church

A missionary is preaching to a few villagers through an interpreter. Nnadi is eavesdropping at some distance.

Priest

Good evening, my brothers and sisters. I have come to bring to you the good news of the word of God, Creator of all things.

Interpreter

(Obsequiously)

Fada him say him white but him black.
Him be broder him be sister. *(Bows at priest)*

Priest

God the Almighty, the only one and living God, Creator and Originator of all living things and of the universe, is breathing his breath upon this village through us, His meek and humble servants.

Interpreter

(Aside to audience)

Nnae! Dat one no eazi . *(Then to villagers)* Fada him say dat God wey him be be na him be,
and na so him go be. *(Bows at priest)*

Priest

God has commanded that we reproach you of this village for worshipping false gods, gods of wood and stone. The true God who liveth on high is neither of stone nor of wood, but of flesh and blood. It is from Him that everything proceeds, and to Him that everything returns.

Interpreter

Fada him say make all wuna, wuna come for him. Wuna bring him plenty good tin. If na goat, wuna bring am. If na fowl, wuna bring am. Him go tell God for heaven for bless wuna: plenty blessing for man wey him bring plenty tin for Fada, small blessing for man wey him konto.

Villager

(Rising)

Ask him say na who be dis him god? Him be Ani wey

67

na we ert god or na Amadioha we na him di bring tonda?
As him dat question make a hier. *(Nnadi listens with greater interest)*

Interpreter
(Whispers to priest)

Priest

All the gods you have named are not gods at all. They are gods
of deceit who tell you to kill your fellow brothers and destroy
innocent children. There is only one true God, and He has the
earth, the sky, you and me and all of us.

Interpreter

All dat wuna god dem no bi god dem. Di only god na dat one
wey fada sey Him dey.

Villager

As him sey if we lef wi god we follow him own god, who
go protect we from dis wi own god dem?

Interpreter
(Whispers to priest)

Priest

Your gods are not alive and cannot do you any harm.
They are pieces of wood and stone.

Interpreter

Fada say dat wuna god dem no bi god dem.
Dem no fit do wuna natin.

Nnadi
(To audience)

Hei?

Villager
(Laughing derisively)

Amadioha!

Villager

Idemili!

Villager

Ani!

Villager

No fit do natin?

Priest and Interpreter
(Singing and clapping their hands)

We have come!
We have come!
To bring light and joy
where darkness and fear
our brethren enchained.

Jesus has said
we should come
and free from the chains
of ignorant blight
the loved ones
of God

(Nnadi listens enthralled, then jumps in dancing. The other villagers rise and join in. Two osu sidle in and fit themselves uneasily among the worshippers, to general movement, first of disbelief, then of protest)

Priest
(In a gesture of appeasement)

Dear Brothers and Sisters in
Christ! Before God there is no slave or free person. We are
all children of God, and we must receive these our brothers.

1st convert
Ha! Ha! No be so. You no understand. If Umuofia see Osu
here, we don die! Dem go laf we kwatakwata.

Priest
Let them laugh. God will laugh at them on judgment day.
Why do the nations rage and the peoples imagine a vain thing? He
that sitteth in the heavens shall laugh. The Lord shall have them in
derision.

2nd convert
Dis palava trong. Osu?

1st convert
Dem no fit marry free-born. Dem no fit attend meeting for
free-born. Na title sef dem fit take?

69

3rd convert

When dem die, na so so oda osu de bury dem.

1st convert

And na for Evil Forest o!

2nd convert

How dat kind people dem fit follow Christ?

Priest

They need Christ more than you and I.

1st convert

If na so, I go go me back for my people. *(Tries to leave but is checked by Nnadi)*

Nnadi

You cannot go back there.

Priest

(Catching both osu by their bushy hair)

Unless you take

off this mark of your heathen belief, I will not admit you into the church. You fear that you will die. Why should that be? How are you different from other men who shave their hair? The same God created you and them. But they have cast you out like lepers, against the will of God. The heathen say you will die if you do this or that and you are afraid. They also said I will die if I build my church on this ground. I am still alive. The heathen speak nothing but falsehood. Only the word of our God is true. Go! And henceforth count yourselves amongst God's chosen children. *(To Nnadi)* Man, what is your name?

Nnadi

Nnadi … Nnadi Egbebuzo.

Priest

God has breathed His spirit on you. From now hence you shall be called Peter.

(Exit converts except Nnadi, clapping)

Priest

Why are you not leaving?

Nnadi

I want us to talk. This my new name.

Priest

Peter?

Nnadi

Yes. What does it mean?

Priest

Why do you ask?

Nnadi

In our tradition a name must mean something.

Priest

In ours too. The name I've given you means rock.

Nnadi
(Pensively)

Rock, rock.

Priest

Big stone.

Nnadi

Stone? Like the one on the barren place we gave you?

Priest

Exactly. That's where you and I are right now. I broke that big stone and used its small parts to build the foundation of this house.

Nnadi
(Rising and inspecting the house with admiration)

Chei! This
your house is strong. We did not know that we could use stones to build our own house.

Priest

It is not my house. It is the house of God. That's why I gave you the name. You are the rock. The rock of God.

Nnadi
(Jubilantly)

I must go and celebrate. I will throw a feast and thank Amadioha and Idemili.

Priest
(Emphatically)

No! no! Not those ones. The only God you should thank is the One in whose house you are. He gave you this name so that you

71

should serve Him.

Nnadi

Serve him? Umuejima!

Priest

(Struggling to pronounce the same word)

Eumeu-ejima. What's that? Another word for God?

Nnadi

No. Twins. Twin children. My own.

Priest

Oh, I see. So you have twin children. You must be a very lucky man indeed!

Nnadi

Not in Umuofia. I was not even allowed to see them.
Clutching his head) They were carried to the Evil Forest.
In sacks. And abandoned there.

Priest

What?

Nnadi

Deep in the forest, eight moons ago. And yesterday…just yesterday
…the owl cried again.

Priest

There is work for you, Peter. Twins must live and owls must be silenced.

Nnadi

Yes, Father…the owls must be silenced.

Curtain

Scene 6

In Okonkwo's house

Desolate air. Okonkwo is seated, head stooped, hitting ground listlessly. Enter Nnadi in buoyant mood. Bends to catch Okonkwo's look but latter turns head away. Nnadi breaks into newly-acquired Christian song.

Okonkwo
(Turning to face Nnadi)
Has your own Mbaino madness too started?

Nnadi
Yes! A healing madness. You will do with some.

Okonkwo
Some what?

Nnadi
Some of my madness.

Okonkwo
You need to be washed in Miniwekwu.

Nnadi
I've already been washed clean.

Okonkwo
But the Oracles have not said so.

Nnadi
Mine is the Supreme Oracle: Jesus.

Okonkwo
Amadioha! Your sanctuary has been re-named.

Nnadi
Not re-named. Destroyed!

Okonkwo
Not destroyed. The massive slab is still there at the Cave entrance.

Nnadi
The rock, you mean? That rock is God's new dwelling place. The cave-dwellers are imprisoned, forever.

Okonkwo
Nnadi, ever since those your people who talk through their noses

73

entered this village, a strong fever has caught your head.

Nnadi

Never mind. Call me Nwoye.

Okonkwo

That cold ash? I have disowned him.

Nnadi

Why?

Okonkwo

He has abandoned my footsteps. He now goes about like a mad child.

Nnadi

What you call madness is but a new inner light. You say a strong fever has caught my head. That is true. Today it's only a few of us, but it will not be long before it becomes an epidemic. Already it's in your own home.

Okonkwo

(Rising)

Amadioha forbid! Not in my house. I will fling out all signs of him. Curse on his head. We will throw all you sick ones into the river...one by one.

Nnadi

Praise be that day when we shall see the new river of life, the cool waters of Jesus Christ.

Okonkwo

(Fixing Nnadi)

Ogbuefi!

Nnadi

Oko!

Okonkwo

I've lost you.

Nnadi

To Jesus! You too need to lose yourself. Our Priest told us something. He said he who loses his life shall find it. You must lose your life to find it. This is why I came. I told you to stay away from Ikemefuna's death. You cut him down.

Okonkwo

(Sharply)

The gods! The gods did!

Nnadi

Leave the gods alone! A god that smites his own child is no god. Yesterday it was Ikemefuna. Before him my twin children. And before them many, many albino children. For how long shall we continue to offend God?

Okonkwo

Not when we do their will. If I hadn't killed Ikemefuna I would be ruined by now.

Nnadi

And now that you killed him, are you not?

Okonkwo

How's that?

Nnadi

Look at your compound. Just yesterday you had many wives and children. Where are all of them now? Ikemefuna was your luck, your health. You lost many things in that one act. This is why I came. You need to join us. Give your soul and body to Jesus. Let him show you a new road in life. Peace be with you. *(Exit)*

Okonkwo

(Alone onstage)

Nnadi and this his sweet tongue. Do this, do that. If I only listen to him I will take an axe and destroy all our shrines. And then where will I go from there? To that his own obasinjom? *(Pensive)* But my wives. My children. My farms. Where are they? Was Ikemefuna a spirit child? Many children like him have been killed in this village before and their death has brought prosperity to their killers. Why is my own turning out this way? His voice rings in my head. Rings more and more. Is he not yet resting? Rest, Ikemefuna. Rest, so that I too may find rest. *(From offstage. Ritual gongs)* Bad tidings. What can have brought out the gongs? Are the gods weeping? *(Making for exit)* The shrines must be quaking. These are not good gongs. *(Hooting of owls)* The owls are crying. *(Sudden silence)* The owls are silenced.

(Exit)

(Curtain)

Scene 7

Village square
Elders are gathered, their mood visibly angry, except for Nnadi's.

1st elder
The sacred python!

Okonkwo
(Raging with fury)
That gang! They will be chased out of
this village with whips! We will whip their wrinkled buttocks
until all the flesh peels off! Kill the sacred python? How?
They must go! They will go! The gods have seen enough!

2nd villager
(More calmly)
Okonkwo has expressed the anger in all our
hearts. But we should not forget the path of reason. It is not
our custom to fight for our gods. If a man kills the sacred
python in the secrecy of his hut, the matter lies between
him and the god. We did not see it. If we put ourselves
between the god and his victim, we may receive blows
intended for the offender.

Okonkwo
Let us not reason like cowards. If a man comes into my
house and shits there on the floor, what do I do? Do I clap
for him? No! I feed him with his own shit, then I take a
stick and break his head. That is what a man does. These
people are daily pouring filth on us, and Okeke says we
should pretend not to see.
(Takes his seat in an open air of disgust)

3rd Elder
Okonkwo has spoken the truth. We shall do something.
But let us cast out these men. We would then not be held
accountable for their abominations. *(Receives nods of accent from all
the other elders. Only Okonkwo shakes his head in disapproval)*

Okonkwo
Are you women, or men who stand up when making water?
What are we discussing? Death of the man who killed the

76

sacred python? Is that something we should be discussing?
I will destroy the beast. He cannot kill our religion and live.

Elders

Amadioha forbid! He cannot! He must not!

Nnadi

Elders of Umuofia, beware of wrestling matches you cannot win.
And you Okonkwo, I have always told you to travel with the sun.

Okonkwo

Nnadi, since when did you become a wrestler? Even the
last mbutuku in this village can throw you. *(Defiantly)*
Enoch will be killed, and by me!

Nnadi

Okonkwo, if you raise your hand against Enoch, God will strike
you down and you will bring a life curse on the village.

Okonkwo

Which god are you talking about? Amadioha, or Mini Weku,
or Ani? It is their will I am doing.

Nnadi

These names you call are not gods.

Villagers

(In a violent outburst of collective anger)
Madness! This is madness! Nnadi has gone mad!
(They all rush at him)

Nnadi

(Undeterred) Stop. I say stop! *(Villagers freeze)* The heathen speak
nothing but falsehood. Only the word of our Lord is true!

1ˢᵗ villager

He has started speaking like the white man.

Nnadi

Yes, I speak like the white man. And you laugh at me now
the way you laughed at him yesterday. But it is yourselves you
should be laughing at.

Okonkwo

Hear him. I told you this Nnadi you see here has gone mad.

Nnadi

Okonkwo, you are still too blind to see. When you finally open
your eyes it may be too late.

Okonkwo

I prefer to die a blind man rather than see the new madness
that has overcome you. Have you swallowed the dirty liquid
of a woman or what?

Nnadi

These are words of destruction. You men of Umuofia, hear me.
When the white man came you laughed at him. You gave him a
barren place with a big rock on it. But he broke the rock and used
it to build the foundation of his church. Today his church is strong,
stronger than all your shrines put together. (*Amid noisy protest from
villagers*)
Yes, his church is strong because it is founded on a rock,
the proverbial rock of God. You too must learn to see value in
everything that God has given you. God gave you a forest but
you transformed it into an evil place where you abandon twins
and albinos. That's not what God said you should do with His
forest and His children. You who have thrown away your children,
Children God gave you out of His bounty, you must repent and
seek His forgiveness. (*Villagers start moving away one by one until he is
left alone onstage*) The forest is crying.
The owls are crying. The twins must live. The twins will
live. And the owl shall be silenced. (*Addressing audience
as he sees that he is alone*) Where are they? They have
returned to their evil ways. But the owl must not cry again.
The white man has come to stay.

Curtain

Scene 8

In the D.C.'s office.

He is seated with a messenger by him. Enter elders armed with machetes. The D.C. receives them politely. They put down their bags and machetes and sit down.

D.C.

I have called you because of what happened during my absence. I have been told a few things, but I cannot believe them until I have heard your own side. Let us talk about it like friends and find a way of ensuring that it does not happen again.

1ˢᵗ villager

What's his name again ?

Okonkwo

Enoch.

1ˢᵗ villager

Yes. My mouth says no to the name. He killed an ancestral spirit under the young sun.

D.C.

Wait a minute. I want to bring in my men so that they too can hear your grievances. James!

Messenger

Saa!

D.C.

Bring in the men.

(James disappears and returns with armed messengers headed by Nnadi)

1ˢᵗ villager

(Trembling with renewed anger)

That son of an osu dared to unmask an egwugwu. He dared to lay his unclean hands on an ancestral spirit.

(Brief scuffle. Elders are handcuffed and taken to a corner)

D.C.

(Rising and pacing the stage.)

We shall not do you any harm if
only you agree to co-operate with us. I have brought you
here because you joined together to molest others, to burn

79

people's homes and their place of worship. That must not happen in the dominion of our Queen, the most powerful ruler in the world. I have decided that you will pay a fine of two hundred bags of cowries. You will be released as soon as you agree to this, and undertake to collect that fine from your people. What do you say to that? (*Elders maintain a sullen silence*). I will leave you for a while. Maybe you need to consult among yourselves. Peter Neidai!

Chief Messenger

Sa! Nnnaaadi, Saa.

D.C.

Answer your name as it is pronounced. Is that clear?

Chief Messenger

Yes Saa!

D.C.

You treat these men with respect because they are the leaders of Umuofia. Your village people, I understand.

Chief Messenger

Yes Saa!

(*Salute by Messengers. Exit D.C.*)

Chief Messenger

(*Smiling wryly into Okonkwo's face and stroking palm with baton*)
We have met again.

(*Messengers taunt elders for a while*)

Okonkwo

(*Snarling*) We should have killed this one too, and the white man if you had listened to me.

2nd messenger

Who wants to kill the white man? You are not satisfied with your crime but you must kill the white man on top of it. (*Gives some elders a knock on the head*)

3rd messenger

(*Prodding Okonkwo*)
You this mouthy one. All over Umuofia it's you they hear. Okonkwo here, Okonkwo there.
(*Okonkwo is staring at him fixedly, rage burning in his eyes*)
You can look at me for as long as you like. This might be the last time you are looking at anything. The D.C. said you

80

people will pay a fine of two hundred bags of cowries. He meant two hundred and fifty bags. Unless this fine is paid immediately, all of you will be taken to the big white man in Umuru and hanged. Not only you. Your families too will be taken there and lined up and shot.

1ˢᵗ villager

Chineke forbid!

3ʳᵈ messenger

Shut up! Chineke, chineke. You knew chineke. And yet you burnt down the house built in his name. You will pay for that sacrilege.

2ⁿᵈ messenger

Yes, and your great, great, great grandchildren after you.

Chief Messenger

(Barking orders)

District of Umuofia special squad
Atte ...ntion! Close ranks! Stand a...t ease! *(Calmly)*
We are matching the prisoners to the cells. Until their fine is paid, or until they are hanged, they have to be given maximum cell treatment. Special squad officer Okereke Jonas!

Okereke Jonas

Present!

Chief Messenger

Remind the rest of the squad what maximum cell treatment is.

Okereke Jonas

On the spot! No food, no water, no visits. Twelve strokes in the morning, six cracks in the afternoon, lashing of the soles in the evening. Two a.m. crying session. Nine strokes for any dry eye.

Chief Messenger

District of Umuofia special squad! Atte...ntion!
Special squad officer Okereke Jonas!

Okereke Jonas

Present!

81

Chief Messenger

March the culprits out. *(Exit Jonas with elders.*
Enter elder from Umuofia) Ah! I see we have an emissary from the villagers. District of Umuofia special Squad! Stand a....tease!

Ezeugo

Messengers of the white man, the people of Umuofia
send you greetings through me.

Chief Messenger

(Angrily)

What? Messengers? Did you say
messengers? *(Turning to the others)* Who ever told
him we were messengers? The white man calls us
messengers and these bush people too call us
messengers? *(Howling at elder)* Say District of
Umuofia special squad, toothless fool!

2nd messenger

That is too sofisticate for him saa!

Chief Messenger

Let that pass. What brings you here?

Ezeugo

The village heard the news you sent. They put
their heads together and sent me to tell you that they
are ready to pay the fine of two hundred and fifty bags of
cowries.

Chief Messenger

Good. I hope I heard well. Two hundred
and fifty bags of cowries. How soon do they want to
pay?

Ezeugo

There are villagers now in the marketplace with the bags on
their heads.

Chief Messenger

That's good. They can bring them here. Let them
bring the bags direct to me. If the Commissioner sees
them before they reach me all your imprisoned elders
will be hanged, and you along with them. *(Elder starts
walking out but is called back by the Chief messenger)*
Wait. Tell them to bring the fine. When we receive it and

count it and it is correct, we will release your elders. But not today. The Commissioner has ordered four days of special cell treatment for them. So bring the fine and wait for your elders in four days. If you agitate they will be hanged, and you will not be spared. District of Umuofia special squad! Atte...ntion! Forwar....d march! One! One! One!

Curtain

Scene 9

Marketplace
(The village is assembled. The mood is sombre)

Okonkwo
Can you see him?

Ezeugo
Who?

Okonkwo
Egonwanne.

Ezeugo
No. Yes, there he is. Are you afraid he will convince us not to fight?

Okonkwo
Afraid? I do not care what he does to you. I despise him and those who listen to him. I shall fight alone if I choose. I shall wait till he has spoken, then I shall speak.

Ezeugo
How do you know he will speak against war?

Okonkwo
Because I know he is a coward.

Elder
(Rising)
Umuofia kwenu!

Villagers
Yaa!

Elder
Kwenu!

Villagers
Yaa!

Elder
You all know why we are here when we ought to be building our barns or mending our farms. My father used to say to me: whenever you see a toad jumping in broad daylight, then know that something is after its life. When I saw you all pouring into this meeting from all the quarters of our clan so early in the

morning, I knew that something was after our life. (*Pause*) All our gods are weeping. Idemili is weeping. Ogwugwu is weeping. Agbala is weeping, and all the others. (*Stops to steady his trembling voice*) This is a great gathering. But are we all here? I ask you. Are all the sons of Umuofia here with us? (*Deep murmur sweeps through the crowd*) They are not. They have broken the clan and gone their several ways. Our brothers have deserted us and joined a stranger to soil their fatherland. If we fight the stranger we shall hit our brothers and perhaps shed the blood of our clansmen. But we must do it. Our fathers never dreamt of such a thing, they never killed their brothers. But a white man never came to them. So we must do what our fathers would never have done. Eneke the bird was asked why he was always on the wing and he replied: men have learnt to shoot without missing their mark and I have learnt to fly without perching. We must root out this evil. And if our brothers take the side of evil we must root them out too. (*Sudden stir in the crowd. Four messengers appear, led by Nnadi. Okonkwo springs to his feet and stands in their way. The crowd is hushed, transfixed*)

Chief Messenger
(*Ordering*)

Make way!

Okonkwo
(*Barring the way*)

What do you want here?

Chief Messenger

The white man whose power you know too well has ordered this meeting to stop. Special squad officer Okereke Jonas!

Messenger

Present!

Chief Messenger

Arrest this rebel! *Okonkwo cuts Okereke down as he approaches. The other messengers flee amidst the rising confusion. The villagers withdraw one by one, frightened, leaving Okonkwo alone onstage with the body.*

Okonkwo

Women, all of them. I knew that Umuofia would not
go to war. I knew because they let the other
messengers escape. I expected them to break into
action. They broke into flight. And yet I thought I
was fighting their fight. I thought men were still men,
like in the days when I slaughtered Isike men at
war. These were days when men were men.
(Throws his hands about in disgust) Now, look at this.
(Wipes his machete on his cloth and leaves stage)

Curtain

Scene 10

In Okonkwo's compound

A few villagers are sitting wearily about. Enter D.C. ccompanied by two messengers.

D.C.

Which of you is called Okonkwo?

Ezeugo

He is not here.

D.C.

Where is he?

Ezeugo
(Raising his voice)

He is not here!

D.C.

Now, no insolence. If you do not produce Okonkwo forthwith, all of you will be locked up.

Ezeugo
(After consultation with the other villagers)

We can take you to
where he is and perhaps your men will help us.

D.C.

I won't have any of your superfluous words. What do you mean by my men helping you? Take me to Okonkwo right away, and be warned: if you play any monkey tricks you will be shot. *(They move towards the part of the stage where Okonkwo's hanging body is hidden, and Ezeugo exposes it)*

Ezeugo
(Choking with anger)

Here! Perhaps your men can help us bring
him down and bury him. We have sent for strangers from another village to do it for us, but they may be a long time coming.

87

D.C.
(*Inquisitively*)
Why can't you take him down yourselves?

Villager
It is against our custom. It is an abomination for a man to take his own life. It is an offence against the Earth, and a man who commits it will not be buried by his clansmen. His body is evil, and only strangers may touch it. That is why we asked your people to bring him down, because you are strangers.

D.C.
Will you bury him like any other man?

Villager
We cannot bury him. Only strangers can. We shall pay your men to do it. When he has been buried we will then do our duty by him. We shall make sacrifices to cleanse the desecrated land.

Ezeugo
(*Angrily to the D.C.*)
That man was one of the greatest men
in Umuofia. You drove him to kill himself and now he will be buried like a dog. He was my friend and my brother.
(*Clutches his head and sobs*)

Messenger
(*To Ezeugo*)
Shut up!

D.C.
(*Disdainfully*)
Peter.

Messenger
Saa!

D.C.
Take down the body and bring it and all these people to the court.

Messenger
(*Saluting*)
Yes Saa!
(*Exeunt except D.C.*)

D.C.

In the many years in which I have toiled to bring civilisation to different parts of Africa I have learnt a number of things. One of them is that a District Commissioner must never attend to such undignified details as cutting down a hanged man from a tree. Such attention can give the natives a poor opinion of the Queen's representative. In the book I plan to write I will stress this point. Every day brings me some new material. The story of this man who kills a messenger and hangs himself will make interesting reading. One can almost write a whole chapter on him. Perhaps not a whole chapter but a reasonable paragraph, at any rate. There is so much else to include, and one must be firm in cutting out details. Choosing a title for the book hasn't been an easy matter. After much thought, though, I have settled on this one: *The Pacification of the Primitive Tribes of the Lower Niger*

(Enter Nnadi)

D.C.

What brings you back, Peter?

Messenger

The fine, Saa.

D.C.

What about it?

Messenger

The village school, Saa.

D.C.

Brilliant idea. Can two hundred bags of cowries build one?

Messenger

Yes, Saa. Two hundred and fifty bags.

D.C.

Any idea what we can call it?

Messenger

Okonkwo Memorial, Saa.

D.C.

Go take the good news to the village. He certainly died so that things fall in place.

(Messenger salute and exit)

The Will

Characters

Lauretta, Late Libong's widow
Mendi, Libong's son
Anta, Libong's daughter
Ema
Bessoe, Libong's sisters
Diboti
Nwana
Professor Ekoko
Madam Tchouta
Dr Tayong Egbe, Libong Group Executives
Sabitout, Lauretta's servant
Jonathan, Mendi's servant
Spirits

Scene 1

Late Libong's dining room

Its comfort reflects his wealthy status. His portrait is on the wall. Enter Ema and Bessoe. Their bearing and dress are of the learned middle class.

Bessoe
(In admiration.)

Good taste.

Ema

Yes, very good taste.

Bessoe

Tells what kind of man he was.

Ema

The quiet colours, the neat patterning of things He had an ordered view on life.

Bessoe

My father always cited him as an example.

Ema
(With some regret.)

Oh, not mine. He was not one to give credit where it's due.

Bessoe

Libong was affectionate.

Ema

Yes, and society loved him for it.
(Brief silence.)

Ema

Emm! Don't you think we ought to call out? Nobody seems to know we are here.

Bessoe

Is anybody around at all? Maybe Lauretta has taken her girl out of town for a rest.

Ema

Leaving the house unattended? I'll try calling out. *(Moves towards exit and calls into backstage.)* U! uuuuu! *(Turning to Bessoe.)* Response! Voices in the back quarters.
(Enter Sabitout. Something of a simpleton. Small apron, big shorts, awkward gait.)

Sabitout
(Wiping hands on apron.)
Are you knock we door womans? We no answer but wunna enter?

Bessoe
(Irritated.)
Why does Lauretta continue to keep this specimen? Ever such an em…

Sabitout
(Cutting in sharply.)
Wuna wan who? I get work for backside eh!

Ema
(Imploringly.)
Sabitout! Are you seeing us for the first time?

Sabitout
Fes tam na which wan?
Since my massa die are you come here? Answer me.

Bessoe
(Harshly.)
Get us your mistress!

Sabitout
(Startled.)
Wandas! Wandas! Aright ma! *(Exit.)*

Bessoe
What an embarrassment!
Can't count the number of times I have asked Lauretta to show this imbecile the door

Ema
She knows why she keeps him though you and I may not.
(Enter Anta.)

Anta
Auntie Ema! Auntie Bessoe! What a surprise. I had given up on both of you.

Ema
(Stepping in to check Bessoe's visible irritation)
We're sorry.

Bessoe
(*In forced ease*)
We intended to come earlier, but just far too many things on our hands. (*Tensing up again.*) This your Sabitout here! Brrr!

Anta
Sabitout? Never mind him. Mother and I have been busy sorting out father's papers.

Ema
We're deeply sorry.

Anta
Thanks for the sympathy. I don't
know who to blame for this. My
father for abandoning us so soon or death for claiming him so early. We're trying to come to terms with the loss.

Bessoe
No easy matter, for sure. How do you replace a baobab tree?

Anta
I miss him so much.

Bessoe
And with reason. But tell me.
Mendi: still in London?

Anta
No. He returned a few days ago.

Ema
And where is he?

Anta
At the Beach. That's where he spends all his time.

Bessoe
Counting sand?

Anta
Counting and changing girls. Today this one, tomorrow that.

Ema
And the business?

Anta
Business? None of his business.
(*Enter Lauretta with a drooping face, wiping her hands with a white*

96

handkerchief)

Ema
(With some exuberance.)

Ohhh! See how our lady looks!

Bessoe

Reminds me of her wedding night.

Ema

The smile…it still has to return.

Anta

Say it…let her hear it from you. I'm tired repeating it.

Bessoe

With time, with time.

Ema

With time, surely. Robert carried much of it to the grave with him.

Lauretta

I'm in shreds. *(Calls out languidly for Sabitout. All four have been standing. They now sit)*
(Enter Sabitout.)

Lauretta

Drinks, Sabitout... drinks for the ladies.

Sabitout
(In a haughty manner at the ladies.)

Yes?

Lauretta
(Admonishingly.)

Sabi- t-o-u-t
Address the ladies politely. Say:
What can we offer you, Madam?

Sabitout
(Repeating with annoyance.)

What we can offer for wunna… Madams?

Lauretta
(Smiling painfully.)

He likes the English language… but the language does not like him.

Bessoe

The English language picks and
chooses its speakers. (*To Sabitout
with some disdain.*) Fruit juice for
both of us. (*Sabitout marches off*)

Ema

The Will. Have you seen the Will? Hope he left one.

Anta

He did, yes.

Lauretta

Robert was a tidy man.
The Will is in Barrister Ekobena's safe keeping.
(*Enter Sabitout with two glasses of juice.*)

Ema

And why have you not asked for it all this time?

Bessoe

You don't seem to be in any hurry to see how well...

Ema

Or how poorly...

Bessoe

You were provided for.

Lauretta

I didn't have to wait for Robert's death
to know what I meant to him.
He provided generously for my welfare.
But even if we wanted to see the Will now
it would be impossible.
Mr Ekobena is away on a business trip in Pretoria.

Anta

And will be away for a month, I understand.

Bessoe

What a time for a business trip!
He grounds ours and goes off to take care of his own.

Anta

I don't think he's to blame.
The death occurred so suddenly
only God could have foreseen it.

Ema

Let's be patient. One month is not one year.

Bessoe

Nor is it one day.
I just hope he did not forget us in the Will.
Or have I asked wrongly?

Anta

No…not at all Auntie.
But you don't need to worry.
Mine is yours as you know.

Ema

(In affected jealousy.)
And me, where do you keep me?

Bessoe and Lauretta

Where do you keep her?

Anta

(Moving across to Ema's embrace.)
Don't mind them.

Ema

Me? Mind them?
(Bares tongue at the other two in mock provocation.)

Lauretta

Sabitout!

Sabitout

(From offstage.)
E hear oo!
(Bessoe and Ema exchange uneasy looks.)

Bessoe

We shall leave you to your work. *(All four start retreating.)*

Lauretta

Sabitout!

Sabitout

(offstage.)
E hear ooo!

Ema

Has he ever heard the short polite form "Madam"?

99

Bessoe

What an embarrassment!
(*Exit all except Lauretta. Enter Sabitout.*)

Lauretta

Clear the glasses.

Sabitout

I hear.
(*Exit Lauretta. Sabitout collects
glasses to one side and sits at the
far end of the stage, legs crossed.
Flips fingers. Enter dance troupe of
four.*)

1ˢᵗ dancer

(*Spoken lines*):

Barefoot Sabitout!
Bare, like his past!
(*Troupe laughter*)
Bare, like his present!
(*More troupe laughter*).
Barefoot Sabitout!
Will your future too be bare?
Bare
Like your bare feet?
(*Troupe expression of
wonder. Dancers respond
energetically to offstage
bikutsi rhythms.*)

2ⁿᵈ dancer

(*Spoken lines.*)

Grammar Sabitout!
Where is your own language?
The English language you butcher
Is not your own
It vomits you
Like the hausaman vomits porkmeat!
(*Booing by troupe.*)
Where is your own language?
Grammar Sabitout?

What has happened to the language
Of your ancestors
Grammar Sabitout?
(*Collective wonder. Dancers respond to offstage Bamoun
rhythm.*)

3rd dancer

(*Female. Spoken lines to embarrassed glances from troupe*)
Barefoot Sabitout!
Where is your virility?
Where your manhood?
You wear an apron
Like a woman servant
Do you crouch to make water
Like a woman?
(*Troupe laughter.*)
Or you stand tall
And proud
And the breeze caresses
Your thing?

(*Troupe murmurs of approval.
Troupe responds to offstage
benskin rhythms*)

Curtain

Scene 2

Libong Group boardroom
(Meeting in session. All department heads in attendance.)

Diboti
Gentlemen, we shall rise for a minute of
silence *(All rise.)* Thank you. Libong is no
more. But his death is physical or is it not?
(Nods of approval.) He's even more alive
now in the Libong Group of Enterprises.

Ekoko
And more so in its four pillars.

Nwana
Yes, four indestructible pillars,
one being technology.

Ekoko
Another education.

Tchouta
And yet another finance.

Dr Tayong Egbe
All these three pillars supporting the fourth
and central one: Health.

Diboti
You have all spoken well.
Libong Enterprises was one with the Chairman's prototype nation.
Shall we bury his dream with his remains?

All
(Energetically.)
God forbid!

Nwana
It shall live on!

Tchouta
It shall thrive!

Ekoko
Education was the lung of the Chairman's ideal nation.

Nwana

Just as a body with deficient lungs withers and dies
so too does a nation with a sick educational foundation
crumble and rot.

Ekoko

Libong was alert to this danger.

Dr Tayong Egbe

Education to him was knowledge housed in morals
of steel.

Ekoko

The Libong University of Arts, Science and Technology
bodies forth this epithet.
We train students in the sciences and technology,
but we also educate them in the virtues of justice,
ceremony, faith and above all benevolence;
for benevolence is the first of virtues,
the one that stands at the heart of humanity.

Nwana

Benevolence. Yes. Libong was a sterling corporate boss,
But he was before anything else a benevolent man.
The Libong Steel Plant testifies to this benevolence.

All

Yes it does.

Tchouta

The Libong Insurance Group prospers by leaps and bounds
all thanks to our Founder's benevolence.

All

Oh yes!

Dr Tayong Egbe

(*Rising to a spirited performance.*)
Education was the heart of Libong's nation.
That heart was not diseased. It was healthy and vibrant.
It was a heart that took the strain of life's daily challenges
a heart that fed the muscles with clean blood.
What better setting could provide Libong's man
with a healthier heart than the Libong Comprehensive Hospital?

Tchouta
(Aside to Nwana.)

Egbe has a deadly passion
for the Comprehensive hospital.

Nwana

He holds that passion from the late Chairman himself.

Dr Tayong Egbe
(To dimmed lights.)

Only Michael Turnball came before
me at Albert's Medical School Queensborough.
AMS is to English medicine what MIT is to American technology.
Michael's name came before mine
but I was not angry: Michael was English, I was not.
So when his name came before mine, a saying crossed my
mind: As an African you have to be superior to be equal.
And even when you are superior equality remains elusive,
like a mirage. No. I was not angry. I was proud.
They wanted me to stay but I said no.
I pointed to the records placing me first.
I could not stay. Not in a country that changed my
first place into second.
So I came home.
Mr Diboti here knows.

Diboti
(Excitedly.)

Yes! Yes! I welcomed him at the airport.

Dr Tayong Egbe

Robert Libong and my father Egbe Tayong Egbe
were classmates and friends.
The day my father offered a reception in thanksgiving
for my safe return home his friend Robert Libong was there.
When I saw him I liked him.
He looked to me like a benevolent man.
And when later in the evening he talked to me
I knew he was indeed a benevolent man.
(Softly.)
My son, he says to me, you have come back
and I am glad. As he speaks his right hand pats me softly

on the back. My friend your father is a good man
And I know you are a good boy.
I will give you charge over my hospital.
Run it, not for me, but for the blood that runs
in all human veins. Run it knowing that blood has but
one colour. Prove to mankind that blood and breath are one
at all times and in all places.
(*Full lights. Takes seat, wiping forehead with handkerchief.*)

Diboti

Dr Tayong, your words crystallise the memory of our
Chairman into a concrete presence. Dear friends, the different
compartments of the Libong Group of Enterprises are alive and
strong. They are alive with the breath of late Libong's dream.
(*Bowing his head.*) But the man is dead. We are left with his dream to
keep alive.

Tchouta

The Chairman did not die intestate, did he?

Nwana

He couldn't have. He was too much of a careful man
to leave the fortunes of his life's dream to chance.

Diboti

He left a Will.

Ekoko

Do we know its exact stipulations?

Diboti

We don't. We can't just yet. The custody of that
very important document was entrusted to Barrister Ekobena.

Nwana

But Ekobena is away in South Africa just now.

Diboti

Yes, and he will be gone for another month or so.
Whatever the case, and pending the release of the Will
let us continue to manage the affairs of the Group
as if our Chairman was still with us.
We shall rise.

Curtain

Scene 3

Libong's house

(Anta is reading and Lauretta is dusting her late husband's portrait. Lauretta holds portrait affectionately. Anta catches her and smiles but does not comment. Lauretta kisses portrait, places it back on the wall and stands staring at it in lost contemplation.)

Anta
(In mild reproach.)

Mother!

Lauretta
(Languidly.)

Yes, my daughter.

Anta

Are you seeing that portrait for the first time?

Lauretta

My daughter, it's just as if I was.

Anta

Since father left us only a few weeks ago
you have dusted that portrait four times every single day
and spent a minimum of two hours each day staring at it.

Lauretta

My daughter, you cannot understand.
Someday, maybe, you will understand.
The day a man takes total control of your life
you will understand.
The day a man eats and you are full
you'll understand. You'll understand
the day a man drinks and you get drunk.

Anta

I understand, Mother. But now you need to come to terms
with the reality of father's eternal absence.

Lauretta

Absence? Did you say absence? Forever?
Robby cannot be gone from me forever. *(Staring at portrait.)*
Not with that smile following me everywhere, everyday.

Anta
(Placing warm hand on mother's shoulder.)
Mother, what you call a smile is but dead pencil strokes
on dead paper.

Lauretta
That's too much torture for my mind.

Anta
Dear Mother, torture, like pleasure, is a permanent feature
of life. Now is the time for you to catch the silver lining.
Pluck it. Give new resolve to your life.
That's one way, the only way even
for you to honour your late husband's smile.
*(Enter Mendi in baggies and cap, beach towel round neck. Throws
himself on a chair and stretches out his legs. Mother and sister watch in
grateful excitement)*

Mendi
(Some air of irritation about him.)
Do people here not know the profits in swimming? On my holidays
on the Spanish Riviera I was alone among white people on the
beach. Here in what passes off for my own country I am still
alone among white people on the beach. Can these people for
once stand up and assert themselves? What place of primeval
darkness is this? *(Haughtily at Anta)* Pair of slippers.

Lauretta
(Confounded)
Get your brother the pair of leather slippers
your father liked so much. *(Exit Anta. Hesitantly, with motherly
affection.)*
My son, since you returned we have not sat down to talk.

Mendi
(Heartlessly.)
Talk? What is there for you and me to talk about?

Lauretta
Your father's estate, your social life, so many things, my son.

Mendi
These things are secondary. For now I am enjoying myself. I hang
out with the girls. My father's business is there to provide the
money.

Laurette

But you need to take care of the estate.

Mendi

That's not my role. I reap. I don't sow. Serve me lunch. Pork chop and chips.

Bordeau. White. Peaches for dessert.

Lauretta

My son, peaches are rare and expensive here.

What about… bananas?

Mendi

(Harshly.)

Peaches!… get them! I knew there were bananas here
but I want peaches.

(Enter Anta with slippers. Places them at his feet and he shows her his canvass shoes. She pulls them off without any sign of annoyance and takes them offstage.)

Lauretta

(Dismayed.)

Mendi, couldn't you have… taken off those shoes
yourself?

Mendi

Ha!…ha!…ha!…With women around? What else are they good for?

Lauretta

You know better.

Mendi

I certainly do. *(To Anta who is just entering)* I'm having peaches
for lunch dessert. I understand they require some looking for.

(Mother and daughter exchange looks. Mendi, sneeringly.)

Peaches are rare and expensive. What about bananas?

(Then mockingly at them)

I see this place is still in the monkey age.

(Enter Sabitout, apron tied upside down.)

Sabitout

(Responding to Lauretta's accusatory look)

I di waka 15 kilometer for kam work, you sabi no, ma.

108

Lauretta

Can you at least wear your apron correctly?

Sabitout

Weti?

Lauretta

Your apron.

Sabitout

(*Looking at apron.*) O! ho! Sorry ma. Na woli.
(*Changes it into place.*)

Mendi
(*Spitefully*)

This one again!

Sabitout
(*Offended*)

Na me he have call dis one? Who be ye?

Lauretta
(*Reproachfully.*)

I've always warned you about impoliteness.

Sabitout

No be for dis one.   He have kush me! I no *fit* lef am!

Lauretta

Sabitout if you don't stop immediately I will fire you.

Sabitout
(*Conciliatorily*)

Solli sa…solli.

Mendi
(*Scornfully at Sabitout*)

Don't you just direct your primitive
mouth at me.

Sabitout

Thank you Sa!

Mendi
(*To Anta as he is about to exit*)

At the same time
as you get my lunch ready, summon the Group Executive
here for a meeting this afternoon. (*Exit*)

109

Lauretta

(At Sabitout angrily)

I don't know what I will do to you and your careless manners.

Sabitout

Na God gi me ma.

Lauretta

Say "Madam", you…

Sabitout

Madam!

Lauretta

I'm going for peaches. You see to lunch. *(Exit.)*

Sabitout

(Questioningly.)

Pieces… pieces na which one?
Na pieces I go cook?
(Sits at far end of stage, legs crossed. Flips fingers. Enter troupe in different costume.)

1st dancer

(Spoken line.)

Yesterday they drank from a cool stream.

2nd dancer

(Spoken lines.)

Today their tongues hang
Scorched by the baking sun.

3rd dancer

(Spoken lines.)

Just yesterday the trees bent
With juicy fruit.

4th dancer

(Spoken lines.)

That was yesterday.
Today the trees starve and die

1st dancer

(Spoken.)

The winds are not good.

2ⁿᵈ dancer

Not good. No, they are not good.
They bring dust, not rain. Dry dust.
Dust that seals the throat like shoe-gum!

4ᵗʰ dancer

No rain about. The rains will be long. Very long.
*(All break into mourning groans as they dance to
doleful mangambeu rhythms. Sabitout throws
in his awkward steps as well. Exit dancers except Sabitout.
Enter Libong Group Executive)*

Sabitout

Wunna kam fine.

Diboti

Get us your Master.

Sabitout
(Searching mind)
Ma massa? Ma massa have die. Wuna no hea ?

Diboti
(With compassionate smile)
Not your big Massa. The new one.

Sabitout

New Massa...New Massa *(Then victoriously)* Massa Mendi?

Diboti

Yes, Master Mendi.

Sabitout
(Yelling into backstage)
Massa Mendi! Massa Mendi! Massa
Mendi oo!
(Enter Mendi)

Mendi
(Rebuking)
What on earth is the matter with you?

Sabitout
(Pointing at guests)
Na people Sa. They has come for see you.

Mendi
(Shows him out sternly, then casually to stunned and abused guests)
Sit down. You are here to examine my welfare. To begin with I left

111

a slate of £4000 in London…restaurant bills and other sundry expenses.
That'll have to be cleared. Right away.

Diboti

Sir….but?

Mendi

Yes?

Diboti

The Will, Sir.

Mendi
(Mockingly)

I'm all ears.

Diboti

Don't you think we ought to wait for it?

Mendi
(With emphatic slowness.)

I-I-I- am the Will. *(Then flaring)*
What effrontery!
(Rising and banging the table.) I am the man in this family.
The only, you may wish to know. My father's wealth is mine
as surely as this *(nudging Diboti's head)* yam on your shoulders
is your head.

Diboti
(Clutching his head in agony.)

Mr Mendi, Sir.

Mendi

Yes?

Diboti

Barrister Ekobena will be back soon. A little pa…

Mendi

Enough of it! Ekobena can be returning only to confirm
the one … in…con…tro…ver…tible truth:
That all my father's estate has been willed over to me.
(Closing in on him.) Could it be any different, Mr Diboti? *(Then moving away)* What kind of world do you live in?
What right-thinking man will
abandon his fortunes to the vagaries of a woman?
That sex is enough trouble already as it is.

My father cannot… repeat… cannot… have committed
such an outrage against common sense.

Diboti

Your London debts shall…

Mendi

Will! Mr Diboti! Will!

Diboti

Yes Sir. Will be cleared on …

Mendi

Now! Mr Diboti! Now! …and my comfort here
must be the object of maximum and permanent concern.

Diboti

On the understanding, Sir, that such concern
meets the spirit of the Will.

Mendi

The Will again. Attach to it what proviso you will!
But do as you are told. And talking about doing as you are told,
the BMW agent will be delivering a Model 600 EFI to me
this afternoon.
(*Catches Tchouta and Nwana as they exchange lost looks. Closing
in on them with disdainful emphasis*)
E…F…I. You cannot know it. Like much else about you,
your knowledge of cars froze in 1940. You are pure
accidents in modern history.
Electronic Fuel Injection. (*Thunderous laughter, then more
quietly*) Electronic Fuel Injection. That's the magic you
are crumbling under. (*Turning to Diboti.*)
Ensure an immediate down- payment of 32 million francs.

Ekoko

(*Echoing the general surprise.*)

But Mr Mendi, Sir, the Group's
resources will be over-burdened.

Mendi

None of my worries. My father was worth more.
I belong among the rich… and keeping me there
is your collective duty.

(*Makes to leave but returns.*)

And talking about keeping me there.

finalise arrangements with the real estate agent
for my residence. I've already chosen one
complete with swimming pool and tennis courts.
400 million francs. Clear that as well.

Sabitout
(From backstage)
Massa Mendi! Massa Mendi! Massa Mendi oo!

Mendi
This is madness incarnate ! *(Sabitout rushes in)*. You must be mad!

Sabitout
No bi me, Sa…. na telephone…. e di ringing !

Mendi
(Knowingly)
That must be Clara. *(Shows Sabitout out sternly.*
Then to Diboti and group) My welfare. That's your duty
morning, afternoon, evening. I'm off to the beach.
(Haughty exit to general stupefaction).

Diboti
(Still stunned.)
How can order beget such chaos?
(Troubled pause)

Ekoko
Libong was a dream. His son the negation
of that dream.
(Troubled pause)

Tchouta
Father lived to build, son to destroy.
(Troubled pause)

Nwana
Mendi came from England, blizzard in mouth
to exterminate the candle of progress
lit by his father.

Diboti
(Dolefully)
The candle is gone, killed. Here we are
plunged into darkness of the darkest kind.
Libong's legacy cannot survive this demonic
haemorrhage.

(Despondent pause)

Dr Tayong
But must we abet such recklessness?

Tchouta
We owe our late Chairman's memory the duty to
protect his legacy from the inferno of his son's
satanic charge.

Diboti
You speak well, you both. But mind you
it was ever Mr Libong's wish that every one
of his son's indulgences be satisfied.

Dr Tayong
Yes. But that was before the demon seized hold
of his soul. His present demands are satanic. Cruel.
They are poised to bury the Group.

Tchouta
And us with it.

Diboti
If such is his will, *(throwing file to seat by him)* then so be it.
When a disaster must happen, it must.
Besides, disasters, too, have their usefulness.

Dr Tayong
My dear friends, the Libong Group are like the Sphinx. If they
die today, out of their death will be born a stronger Group.
*(Crestfallen exit. Enter Sabitout, attracted by sudden silence.
Picks file and opens. Enter Mendi.)*

Mendi
(Asking for file, abused)
Not for your illiterate hands.

Sabitout
(Handing over file)
Thank you Sa.

Mendi
And where are they?

Sabitout
They has go, Sa.

Mendi
Now, you get lost and call in Jonathan as you disappear.

115

(Exit Sabitout. Enter Jonathan)

Jonathan

The caddy has just been here, Sir. Says the golf session is at four this evening.

Mendi

Good. I'm dining out today, at the Golf Club.

Servant

Yes Sir. *(Makes to leave, then returns)* And your dinner, Sir. It's already cooked.

Mendi

Let the dogs have that.

Servant

Yes, Sir. *(Moves to drink corner.)*

Mendi

Jonathan.

Jonathan

Sir.

Mendi

A shot of whisky.

Jonathan

Yes Sir. *(Pours shot and takes towards him.)*

Mendi

Make it two.

Jonathan

Yes Sir. *(Pours second shot and takes towards him)*

Mendi

Three…make it three.

Jonathan

Yes Sir. *(Pours third shot and takes it to him. Returns to drink corner)*

Mendi

(Moves over to phone. Picks up receiver. No tone. Drops receiver, dejected)
Three days to get London and still no speck of a chance…*(holds up fingers emphatically)* three days… what a jungle.
(Eerie sounds of hooting and flute from offstage. Picks up receiver and dials, face creased. Drops receiver in disgust. Continues monologue amid dim offstage sounds.)
What age are we in for the sake of me? Is this not the communications age? The digital age? And this blighted

corner of the earth pursues its deep slumber in the age of the talking drum... the crier...the errand man....*(With rising voice)* I cannot send an errand man to London.... It will take him four hundred years to get there... and which direction will he go to start with?...*(Derisively)* Post offices? One would sooner run to London than post a letter there from this bleak place.

(Orders servant over with whisky. Servant pours him some. He takes a few absent-minded sips, puts down glass and moves to forestage.)
There's something about this place that numbs my thinking. In this place light is not light; it is something else; something not very unlike darkness. This place delights in darkness...swears by darkness...worships darkness. *(Returns to his seat. Servant moves over to him.)*

Jonathan

Some more whisky, Sir?

Mendi

(Dismisses servant with wave of hand.)
In London I was washed in light. I saw light and was guided by it. When you are lit by light you cannot but see your way... and seeing your way means moving forward...in the right direction. In light things are clear...transparent. Governed by light, society becomes human... it has a face...not a hideous mask. It doesn't grower at you *(mimics)* like a Frankenstein monster. Darkness is the devil's curse, light man's gift from God. I am here in this dark place...here...in this place of darkness...this place of evil. I can only be bad. I will destroy. I will annihilate. I will be the devil's messenger, agent of evil, evil's most dreaded instrument. *(Shoots out his glass for more whisky. Servant fills it and he pours it down in one stretch. Howling in visible drunkenness as he staggers to eerie sounds once again.)* The dark place! I will bring everything to naught! I will ruin....ha!...ha!...ha!...ruin...Ha!...ha!...ha! *(with quiet purpose)* and ruin even the ruins! *(Convulsive laughter. Enter Lauretta and Anta with sneering faces)*

Mendi

(Dangling on his feet)
And now...you both... still waiting for   the Will? Sounds to me like waiting for Godot, if you know what that means.

Anta

(*In spiteful anger, away from him*)

We shall wait! And shame unto you…destruction incarnate. Curse be the day you entered my mother's womb…a greater curse on the day you were born.

Mendi

(*Unimpressed.*)

Your curse cannot settle on me.
Curse the darkness… the heavy, clotted,
stinking darkness in which your race is lost.

Anta

Darkness has no hand in your plunder and rape of our family heritage. Your mind is cruel…. your hand is wicked… you are a beast!

Mendi

Oh well, but let me tell you. This place is a moral wasteland. And I am not one to preach virtue in the desert.

Anta

A moral greenfield, you mean? But you are seeing it through the scorching blaze of your evil mind.

Lauretta

What pleasure does destruction give you?

Mendi

Anarchy is my drug, destruction my opium. What my father built for I do not know. This blighted spot is not worth a jot of man's constructive energy.

Anta

(*Dragging stunned mother away*)

I will not stand here
to listen to such ignominy.
Curse be the day you were conceived…
a greater curse on the day you were born!

Mendi

(*Moving to forestage with smile on face.*)

There's nothing here of my making.
My father lived out of his age… and out of his world.
He should have been British…or American. He could even have been French…or Italian. This was the wrong

118

place for him. A forest is a sight of competing trees…
not a jumble of stunted growths and lanky climbers.
A baobab in a scorched land stands out, like an elephant
in the savannah. My father was a baobab. Death cut him
down. I will dispose of the trunk… I will
sweep away all traces of his effort…branches and leaves
will go…roots will wither in the parched earth… I will
take away the shade…and the waiting sun will harmonise
the desolation. In the beauty of rolling dunes an
oasis becomes an eyesore. When I am done with my job
I will return to civilisation. I will go where a forest is a
sight of competing trees.

Curtain

Scene 4

Boardroom

(Torn chairs are thrown about the dusty working table. The few members present are tattered, despondent)

Diboti
(Rising and examining members)

I do not know whether
 to call you... gentlemen... or paupers.
Each one will choose his title.
(They all throw embarrassed glances at one another, then at themselves.)

Tchouta

Paupers. We can only be paupers.

Ekoko

See how rich my clothes are.

Nwana

And mine!

Tayong

And mine too. Very rich!

All

Paupers!
(Prolonged collective laughter, then silence)

Diboti

A holocaust would not have done better. The waste is spectacular.
(Pause)

Tayong

I am shaken to my very bones.
(Pause)

Tchouta

I am terrified.
(Pause)

Nwana

So devils wear human faces!
(Pause)

120

Diboti

He has raised destruction to an art… a harrowing art. Libong's memory is abused.

(*Enter messenger with letter. Hands it to Diboti who opens it anxiously.*)

Diboti

It's from Barrister Ekobena…says he returned late last night.

Ekoko

(*Anxiously*)

And the Will. Any mention of it?

Diboti

No. He is silent on it.

Tayong

We need to know.

Nwana

We have to know. All our hopes are in that Will.

Ekoko

What difference does it make now what the Will says? The deed has been done. The Will comes a bit too late.

Tchouta

No! Worse situations have been rescued. It's not yet too late. Libong left us with his vision. His goals were clear, the road to them straight. What we need now is someone to incarnate that vision, to bring it alive again.

Diboti

What if the Will confirms Mr Mendi's claim to his father's estate…or what is left of it?

Tayong

We shall then know that the estate was meant to suffer this dark fate. But until that is established, I shall continue to believe along with Madam Tchouta that there is still some hope.

Diboti

Barrister Ekobena wants to hold discussions with us in the coming days.

Nwana

The sooner the better.

Tchouta

Tomorrow…why not tomorrow?

Tayong
Now...now is the time...and not for discussions but for the Will to be released.

Diboti
He will not be available before three weeks.

Tayong
We cannot wait. Send for him now.

Tchouta
Why send for him? Let's march to his chambers. We need The Will. Our very lives are in it.

All
(*Excitedly, each saying his own.*)

To his chambers! God forbid!

Enough of it!

Diboti
As you will have it, paupers. Let's go! (*Angry exit by all.*)

Curtain

Scene 5

In the Libong kitchen

*Hunger and want hang over the place. Enter Anta. Opens pots
frantically and closes each one in disappointment. Sinks to a stool
and breaks into a sob.)*

Anta

This is the work of death. I never knew hunger. Today it is my
bedfellow. Poverty was a distant story, now I carry it in my
handbag. Oh death! Where is your victory? (*Pause*) But here it is:
those empty pots... the mouldy smell of this kitchen... the
howling worms in my stomach. Who ever said you were not
powerful? You are strong... stronger than the baobab tree...
stronger still than the strongest man. You cut down my father.
(*Growing more hysterical.*) You death! I hate you! I...I...I...
(*Calming down.*) Oh my God. I'm so sad. (*Enter Lauretta.*)

Lauretta

(Throwing her arms around her daughter.)

Anta my daughter!
Your father will not be glad to see you like this. Wasn't it
you who said pain, like pleasure, was a permanent
feature of life? Remember the silver lining? Now is the time
to pluck it and give new resolve to your life. You see, there's
wealth because there's poverty; hunger because there is
plenty. Today it's the bright side, tomorrow the dark.
We must learn to pick up the pieces.

Anta

Mother, some of these things are easier said than done.
You talk about pieces. When did our life shatter into pieces?
What happened? Why? Why did it have to happen only to us?

Lauretta

I wish I could answer your questions. But I am not in God's
mind. All I know is that fate has eyes; and so does destiny.
These messengers of God know their road and how to
travel it. Your father was cut down at the peak of his might.
He was not ill, he was not quarrelsome. God quite simply
said his time had come. Remember he died in his sleep.

(Moves away from her daughter and assumes a grave mood.)
I woke up in the morning and was talking to him from the
bathroom with my toothbrush in my mouth. I was even
angry that he was not answering. It was not like him not to
answer when I talked. I grew angry and raised my voice.
Still no answer. I removed my toothbrush and rinsed my
mouth. Still no answer. Then my body chilled, as if a current
had struck me. I was dumb. I was dead. *(Lowers herself
into a chair too.)*

Anta
(Rising)

Mother, rise to your feet. Since my father died we have
been on our knees. We have suffered. We have been
hungry. We have been thirsty. We have known poverty.
Now is the time for us to pluck the silver lining. Our heads
cannot remain bent forever. Hunger is no calamity
unless it becomes a permanent condition. Poverty is not
a curse unless we wear it like a cloak. We must cast off
the mantle of poverty. We must tie our loincloths and
work. That is the secret… work, work, more work.

Lauretta
(With determination.)

We are back on our feet again.
We must cast out the bad spirit from our midst.

Anta

Yes, even if that bad spirit is housed in my own brother.

Lauretta

A brother is no brother if he does not protect the family
heritage.

Anta

Nor is he a brother if he sets fire to the family bond.

Lauretta

Your father could not have died for nothing.

Anta

No. He died so that we should discover the secrets of life.
I am more mature today. Life is not the garden of Eden
I thought it was. It is a bumpy road. It is a stormy river.
(Enter Bessoe and Ema.)

124

Ema
(Sniffing the air with disgust.)
All the rich smell is gone.
Lauretta, when did you last cook in this place?

Lauretta
I can't remember.

Bessoe
Not even with the return of Barrister Ekobena?

Anta
What has Ekobena's return to do with my mother's kitchen?

Ema
The Will.

Bessoe
Of course, the Will. That's why we've come. *(Pacing up and down.)* We need to know where we stand in that Will.

Lauretta
We have not seen the Will.

Anta
And we are not in the least interested in it.

Ema
(Totally amazed.)
What? You? Not interested in the Will?

Bessoe
Don't mind them. Ekobena has revealed the contents to them and that's why they are saying what they are saying.

Lauretta
Take it whichever way you please, but know that that document will not make me and my daughter any happier than the lesson my husband's death has taught us.

Anta
The Will can only bring us fish. From now on we will catch our own fish.

Bessoe
Can we therefore have your own share of the property?

Lauretta
(Laughing heartily.)
Property? What property? Take it if
you find it. There's no property left. Libong's Estate is
under liquidation.

Bessoe and Ema
What?

Anta
Just as you have heard. Under liquidation. Even the ground we
are standing on no longer belongs to us.

Ema and Bessoe
We must seek the culprit. We shall not be dispossessed.
(Exeunt confusedly.)

Lauretta and Anta
(Laughing)
If only they knew who the culprit was!
*(Enter Mendi, tattered, repentant. Reaches out to mother
and sister as they step backwards in horror.)*

Mendi
(Crying out)
Mother…*(Mother drags daughter towards exit)*
Anta…my sister…*(Mother and sister disappear)* Not
yet…no…don't leave me alone…
(Enter spirits in black. Growl and gnarl at him to psychedelic sounds offstage.)

1st Spirit
(Bending over prostrated Mendi)
Mother. Did you know her
when you came?
(Heightened offstage sound)

2nd Spirit
Sister. Did you know her when you came?
*(Spirits growl. Mendi removes
himself to another stage corner. Spirits follow)*

3rd Spirit
Your father's legacy. Where is it? *(Mendi covers face)*

1st Spirit
Libong's Comprehensive Hospital! *(Mendi goes down on one knee)*

2ⁿᵈ Spirit

The Libong Insurance Group! *(Mendi goes down on the other)*

3ʳᵈ Spirit

The Libong Steel Plant *(Mendi lies prostrate on the ground)*

1ˢᵗ Spirit

The Libong University of Science and Technology!

(Puts foot on Mendi's prostrated stomach, then shouts) Karma! *(Heightened offstage sounds. Shouts again Karma! to fluctuating psychedelic flute and drumbeats offstage. Spirits step aside, fold arms and watch. Mendi starts at each gush of offstage beats. Looks at audience and pulls eyes away. Folds hands on right knee. Unfolds them. Supports one jaw. Brings hands together again. Takes sideways glance at audience. Moves across stage to another seat. Continues confused gestures. Rises, reels, stumbles, falls, rises, slouches forward, clasps head, chest. Crashes to the floor in one final convulsive fit. Offstage sounds fade off into silence. Spirits stand watch over lifeless body).*

Curtain. End

The Imprisonment
of Sende Ghandi

Characters

Sende Ghandi, Corporate banker and purported thief
Laura Ghandi, Wife to Sende Ghandi and Accountant to
Sunday Innocent
Sunday Innocent, Bank Manager
Farmers, Enegembole
Nonobit
Bine
Ewang
Police Commissioner
Police officer
Police constables, Lukong
Ekambi
Guards
Clerk
Sunday's henchmen, Kum
Dragon
Pepper

Scene 1

Public square
(Sende Ghandi, neck in tyre, about to be roasted.)

Dragon

Kerosene!

Kum

Not kerosene! Petrol! Burns faster!

Pepper

Petrol for speedy death!

Dragon

Big thief !

Kum

Shame !

Ghandi

Not me!

Dragon

Rogue !

Ghandi

I've not stolen!

Kum

Liar !

Pepper

Fat liar !

Ghandi

Not me. I beg... in God's name !

Dragon

God eh ? You will be with him...soon. *(Starts pouring petrol).*

Ghandi

In God's name!

Dragon

Lighter!

Kum

(Searches pocket).

Ghandi
(Implores, silently first, then vocally).
I was just passing.

Kum
You were just passing. And this? *(Showing wallet).*

Ghandi
But that's my wallet!

Dragon
(In mock hysterical laughter)
You hear him? He says that's his wallet. He will soon say the money in it is his.

Ghandi
(Goes down on knees and folds hands in supplication).
I have a wife and two children. Their picture is in the wallet. For their sake, please!

Pepper
(Dragging him up).
So that's how you feed them.
You steal people's wallets, then turn round and say they belong to you.

Dragon
Why even bother? He can have four wives and ten children, he'll perish. Let me see. *(To purported thief)*
Now, Mr husband, you want to go back to your wife, eh? *(To Pepper)* Pull him this way. *(Pepper drags thief to forestage)* Now dance. *(Hesitation by thief)* Dance I say!
(Thief breaks into improvised dance to no music at all)
(Enter Police Officer and patrol team)

Officer
Stop. No jungle justice.

Pepper
Big thief sa!

Officer
(Inspects thief with interested concern).
Interesting.
Very. Constable Ekambi!

Ekambi
Present!

Officer

March thief to charge office.

Ekambi

And the tyre sa?

Officer

Tyre and all, fool!

Ghandi
(*Protesting*)

I'm not a thief.

Officer

And that? (*Pointing at tyre*). Out with him!
(*Exit Constable Ekambi with Ghandi*)

Officer

You don't burn such good cases. How much?

Dragon

Three million.

Officer

Interesting. Very! (*Taking pensive walk*) Six hundred
thousand.?

Pepper

Whose?

Officer

Yours.

Kum

Too small.

Officer

Take it or leave it. I have the thief.

Dragon

He's our thief.

Officer

He was.

Lukong

Thieves belong to us.

Pepper

But it's from us they steal!

Officer

Interesting. Very.

Lukong

And it's to us they render account.

Officer

Clear. Patrol continues.

(Exit Kum and co. protesting confusedly)

Officer

(To Lukong, pensively)

Constable.

Constable

Sa!

Officer

You see, this is an interesting happening. Very.
There are lessons in it for you. I have a house.
You know it. *(Demonstrating)* Four bedrooms,
three toilets, twin parlour, imported tiles and
glassware…yes! yes! This is how I built it. My mind is always alert,
my eyes always open. I never let a chance pass. You see, I've just
cut 2.4 million. And that's not all for the day. A patrol is no patrol
unless it leads me to wealth. You understand? Money…wealth…
get me? That's what we toil for; nothing else.

Constable

But Sa, I thought we were patrolling to maintain peace
and order.

Officer

Just that…with a little incentive on the side. You have to open
your mind to the chances of life. You march on gold everyday,
and everyday you go home poor. Because your eyes are blind to
the chances of this life, each of your outings is a race into greater
poverty. You see, people may not know it, but there is no such
thing in life as stealing. The biggest lesson I learnt
from my civics instructor at the Police College is that
what people call stealing is just an act of acquisition
interrupted. Out of ignorance, people allow themselves to be
called thieves whereas they should be called
interrupted acquirers .

Lukong
(Reflecting)
Interrupted acquirers…interrupted acquirers…
Interrupted… *(Then triumphantly and with broad gestures to Officer)* Sa, you mean…so…you acquire.
You don't steal.

Officer
Just that. Yes. In life you acquire everything that you possess. You only have to be careful about people interrupting you each time you are in the process of acquiring because some of those interruptions can be brutal, like the one we have just seen.

Lukong
Sa, from tomorrow I too will become an acquirer.

Officer
(Placing friendly hand on Constable's shoulder)
Only, beware of tyres.

Lukong
(Saluting enthusiastically)
Yes Saa!

Curtain

Scene 2

On Ewang's farm.

(Workers, four in number, three men and a woman, enjoying conversation break)

Nonobit
(Laughing)
She thought she was clever.

Bine
Like all of them!

Enegembole
We are oh!

Ewang
His energy.

Nonobit
My energy. Can you work harder than me?

Bine
The money. That's my own cry.

Nonobit
Money? No anini.

Enegembole
Like all of you … hmm!

Nonobit
Only my head. Thirty minutes just before her fat oga.

Bine
(Laughing)
I know that one. With his tattered buttocks and belle like
Mbakwa Supe.

Nonobit
She pushed me out through the back door and he
came in through the front door.

Ewang
But you had taken no?

Nonobit
Ah ah! You are saying it again?

Enegembole

Thieves you two. Take here, take there.
One day... one day you will take from your own
mother!

Nonobit and Ewang

God forbid!

Enegembole

God forbid. God cannot forbid. Did you pay? But see:
the sun is cleaning its hoe.

Bine

Nonobit, you fool us with woman talk.

Ewang

Let him continue. We will be in his farm tomorrow.

Nonobit

Ah! You too! This clearing season is the ripe time
for storytelling. Lightens the work.

Ewang

I prefer the harvest season.

Bine

When the money caresses our hands.

Enegembole

But can you harvest without planting?

Ewang

To your question I give this answer: some plant,
some harvest. You plant today and weed. Weed and
weed. Your palms tear and blood flows.

Nonobit

And sweat dances on your forehead.

Ewang

Sweat sits on your forehead like the cock's dewlap.
But others harvest.

Nonobit

Have you heard? *(All stop working and stare at him).*
Sende Ghandi. Yesterday in the marketplace. They wore
a tyre round his neck to kill him. It was bad.
Then the police came.

Ewang

Sende Ghandi's neck?

138

Nonobit

As you hear. Kum & co. That he was a thief.

Enegembole

Kum & co.! Justice tried!

Ewang

Tyre on the wrong neck ! Not Sende Ghandi. I know his cross. Women. Aita… Sofikoto… Enanga… Sirri…Fat buttocks, thin legs, koni eyes…he is there.

Enegembole

That was before his marriage. Today he has only one cross: our Co-operative Scheme. That tyre round his neck troubles me a lot. Does justice have eyes? Does it see?

Bine

Does it at all? If I am a struggling farmer today, I hold justice responsible.

Nonobit

Yes, Bine, I've not always known you to be a farmer.

Bine

Farming was not in my blood. I'm a supplier.

Nonobit

All the big schools, all the training centres were yours.

Bine

I supplied them food: plantains, meat, okro, ekomobong, congo meat, rice. Then the prisons came. I took all my money and supplied them. You think they paid me any anini? One superintendent after the other, they threatened to lock me up if I continued to ask them for my money. I had to choose between my head and my money. Not even their big oga in the capital could help.

In fact he told me all his men in the field were honest people, that I was lying.

Enegembole

You are lucky they even spared you your life.

Ghandi is in jail for no crime, and if we are not fast they will silence him for always. The pact. Now. *(They all come together and pile right hands, one on the other, then throw the pile outwards to a thundering hurrah)*

Curtain

Scene 3

Co-operative Building

(Manager's office. Enter Accountant Mrs Laura Ghandi with reports for Manager. Settles them before him and disappears to sustained ogling by Manager. Manager, glasses poised on nose, sips coffee. Coffee burns his lips. Puts cup down protesting. Pores over figures, rings bell and Accountant appears again and stands at a respectable distance.)

Mr. Sunday

(Over his glasses and beckoning).

Not so far...closer... come closer. *(Accountant moves closer with professional stiffness. Manager hands her document.)* Yesterday's transactions...let's have them.

Accountant

(Reading from document).

Farmers' deposit: six million
FCFA. Loan requests: nine. Total amount of loan request:
three hundred thousand FCFA. Seeds and fertilizers.
Total amount of loans approved: none.

Mr. Sunday

Beautiful. Sound management eh, Mrs Ghandi?

Accountant

Yes, Sir, except that we could be more farmer
friendly.

Mr. Sunday

How's that?

Accountant

We've been in activity for three months, Sir. Our
total deposits stand at 480 million, but we have not
given out a single franc in loan to farmers.

Mr. Sunday

Lending money to farmers is not our prime objective.

Accountant

But Sir, they put the money here, unless I'm
mistaken.

Mr. Sunday

They do, sure, and we take care of it for them. What did you say our total deposits were?

Accountant

480 million. And this does not include the 275 million in encouragement subsidy from our foreign partners.

Mr. Sunday

So we can boast of a healthy 700 million.

Accountant

755 million, to be more exact, Sir.

Mr. Sunday

Well, precision is not our prime objective here. A difference of only 55 million really doesn't matter, does it, Mrs. Ghandi?

Accountant

We're in banking, Sir.

Mr. Sunday

Sure, sure. 755 million. That's a lot of money. Yes, yes. Now, we cannot keep all this money here.

Accountant

I don't understand, Sir.

Mr. Sunday

I mean, 755 million is quite an amount. We need to branch out …. make deposits in other places. *(Paces up and down, then looks fixedly at Accountant)*. I have opened a bank account in Sweetzerland…in my name. But mind you, it's for the farmers' money. We will transfer the money to that account as it comes in. We can start with a first trial transfer of 753 million.

Accountant

Sir, we will be left with just 2 million.

Mr. Sunday

That's perfectly in order. We don't need more than that here, do we, Mrs. Ghandi? The farmers want 300.000 for seeds and fertilizers. They can buy the seeds on hire purchase and settle their creditors after harvest. As for fertilizers, I don't see what they need them for in a volcanic region like this one. Volcanic soil is rich soil, richer than any fertilizer can match. Mmmm ... Mrs. Ghandi!

Accountant

Sir.

Mr. Sunday

Remember our finance law places the upper limit of unauthorized transfers at 100 million. Beyond that amount you need clearance. So break the money down into innocent bundles of 100 million each time and at all times. In these things you have to be clever.

Accountant

I don't see the justification for such transfers, Sir. Why send all this money to ...

Mr. Sunday

Sweetzerland

Accountant

Switzerland. Why send all this money to Switzerland when we need it so badly here?

Mr. Sunday

Mrs. Ghandi, we are here to keep the farmers' money. Where we do that really doesn't matter, does it? Besides, I cannot sit on such heavy money and that weight is not reflected in my foreign bank account. Let's be realistic, Mrs. Ghandi.

Accountant

You are the Manager, Sir.

Mr. Sunday

(Pause. Then softly.)

Laura! *(Stretches out hand to touch her but she pulls back)*. I don't know why you are always so formal with me. Mr. Manager, Mr. Manager all the time. Call me Sunday. Isn't it so much nicer if I call you Laura and you call me Sunday? You have a very beautiful name.

Accountant

I'm very flattered, Sir, but I prefer to be called Mrs. Ghandi.

Mr. Sunday

(Laughs somewhat mockingly, then rises and holds her).

I love you Laura!

Accountant
(Resisting).

Leave me or I'll scream!
(Bell falls and clerk rushes in.)

Mr. Sunday
(Disengaging with anger, then to clerk).

Get out, you fool!

Clerk
(Backing out.)

I'm sorry Sir. I thought you called.

Mr Sunday
(Waves him out angrily. Clerk disappears. Turning to Accountant who is standing at some distance).

Laura, is it wrong to love you?

Accountant

You are married, Sir, unless I'm mistaken. In any event,
I am.

Mr. Sunday

Well! Well! But don't forget the transfer, first thing tomorrow.

Accountant

I'm not sure it will be appropriate for me to carry out
such business, Sir.

Mr. Sunday

Madam! Those are instructions.

Accountant

Then they will be carried out, Sir! …to the letter. *(Exit
Accountant to renewed ogling).*

Mr. Sunday
(At his table).

I will do what it takes to have you. If
money is the price, I will pay it. Is there any woman on
this earth above 755 million? If Ghandi is the obstacle, I
will clear him! He's already even as good as cleared. Kum
& co. are seeing to that.

Curtain

Scene 4

In charge office.
(Constables Ekambi and Lukong are engaged in game of cards)

Ekambi
Box di tin fine massa!

Lukong
You wan make I box am again how?

Ekambi
Shake di tin again small, massa. Ah! You too! You konto
even for boxin?

Lukong
(Shuffles cards again).
You don glad no? *(Showing pack*
to Ekambi). Cut. James Bond. Addition and subtraction.
(Shares cards and they start playing).

Ekambi
9.

Lukong
5.

Ekambi
I pass. *(Interrupting play).* I say eh, massa, dat Ghandi inside
dey na how? Four days now.

Lukong
Na special case. Chief get deal dey.

Ekambi
Wetin he do self? I beg, serve me card. *(Resumes playing).*
 2.

Lukong
9.

Ekambi
2.

Lukong
7!

Ekambi
Dis one pass me.

Lukong
(Sweeps the stakes)
Kum & co. dem say i tif.

Ekambi
Kum? Kum wey i tif sotay go tif cargo wey i tif am go lefam
for i mami i house? Na i di say anoda man tif? And dat man
na Sende Gandhi? Kontri don spoil. We go wan see here some
day Lyonga di brin Oumarou sey i don tif i shwain.

Lukong
Di matta na 3 million. Na so I hear. And Inspector wan cut 2.4
dey.

Ekambi
I know sey Inspector no di choose.

Lukong
If na you?
(Enter Laura)

Lukong
(To colleague)
Massa! dis one na luck mop.

Ekambi
I go try my chance dey.

Lukong
i dey so you no know your own level. Dis kind wan
na for me.

Ekambi
Because me I no bi man. Aright. Serve me card. If I win
na me I go take i.

Lukong
Lef me dat talk. If I win…if I win. You don ever win me
for card before wey na today i go happen because you
don see fine woman? *(Rising and strolling about
buoyantly)* Listen, my boy. This is not a matter of
winning but of acquiring. This case is for acquirers.
Yes. You walk on gold everyday, and everyday you
return home poor. *(Ekambi stares at him lost)* You have to open
your eyes to the chances of life. By the way, you and I did not
enter Ikeja at the same time.

Ekambi
(Searching mind for reply)

Eh..eh..

Lukong

Don't waste your energy. I left the place before you came in.

Ekambi

Lie! Lie! We did drills together.

Lukong

Never mind. Not the same batch. *(Sitting to a pensive statement)* You see, the biggest lesson I learnt from my civics instructor at the Police College is that what people call stealing is just an act of acquisition interrupted. People allow themselves to be called thieves whereas they should be called acquirers interrupted. Back to the game!

(They get down to a furious game of cards, apparently oblivious to Laura's presence but in fact spurred by it).

Laura
(Somewhat hesitantly)

Good evening. *(No response.*
Repeats greeting). Good evening, Officers.

Lukong
(To Ekambi, flattered)

I di always say I be officer but
you no di gri. You don hear no?

Ekambi

Serve me cards. Na officer man di chop?

Lukong
(Serves last round of cards)

Deal.

Ekambi

(Consulting cards in angry disappointment, then throwing them on the table and disrupting the game).

I no fit gree. i no fit waka so. How you fit carry only mami coco, mami coco you pakam for my hand? *(Then angrily to Laura).* What do you want?

Laura

Ghandi. Mr. Sende Ghandi. Can I see him, please?

Ekambi

There's no… *(Derisively)* Mr. Sende Ghandi here.
There's a thief locked up here by name Ghandi.

Laura

Yes, that's the one.

Ekambi

Is that the man *you* have come to see?

Laura

Yes.

Ekambi

Who is he to you?

Laura

My husband.

Lukong

What?

Laura

My husband, Sir.

Lukong

Who are you calling Sa? Call me Officer.

Laura

I'm sorry.

Ekambi
(To Lukong)

Massa! dis tif people dem di chop fine tin o!

Lukong

Money di buy all tin for dis ground. *(Then to Laura)*.
Are you his wife or his njumba?

Laura
(Calmly)

His wife. We have two children.

Ekambi
(Angrily to Lukong)

Weti you di ask i all dat one for? *(Then
to Laura)*. You cannot see him. He has been moved to a
maximum security cell in the main station.

Laura

But I've just been assured by the Station Superintendent that he is here.

Ekambi

Woman! do you want to teach me my job?

Laura

I'm sorry.

Lukong

You can see him …I mean…but … there are conditions.

Laura

(Visibly relieved)

I will not mind fulfilling them
please. I need to know his condition.

Lukong

We like women like you who cooperate. Some of them come here and fill our ears with sabitout grammar and when their clients die of sickness they start telling all kinds of lies about the charge office. We don't torture detainees here. *(To Laura, with sneering emphasis).*
 If you don't cooperate your husband will *die* …of sickness…this very night. Mind you, this is not a hospital.

Laura

(With growing impatience)

The conditions, please.

Lukong

(Winking victoriously at Ekambi, then addressing him more openly).
Check the consultation room.

Ekambi

But you used it last, just two hours ago. I hope it will be my turn this time. *(Furtively to audience)* Why i di always wan make me op eye? i no fit waka dis time!

Lukong

We can actually take turns.

Ekambi

Na so! When it's your turn you are alone. When it's mine… we take turns. i no fit waka dis time!

148

Lukong

Are you not happy that I even want you to have a bite
of such good meat?

Laura
(Sensing foul play)

What is this talk of turns and meat?

Lukong
(Angrily to her)

Cooperation, not questions, woman.

Ekambi

You either cooperate and see your husband or ask
questions and his corpse will answer them for you
tomorrow.

Laura
(Defiantly)

It will be neither one nor the other! Bunch of scoundrels!

Ghandi
(From offstage)

Laura-a-a!

Laura

Sende-e-e!

Ekambi

Shut up !

Lukong

Shut up, both of you!

Laura
(Making a defiant exit)

You will be hearing from me
soon.

Lukong
(Still stunned)

Massa! you sure sey dis Ghandi na tif man?

Ekambi

i matta? i mus be tif man before wi katch i lockam?
Dat nyango talk again say weti?

Lukong
(Mimicking Laura)

You will be hearing from me soon.

149

Ekambi

I di wait i. i use some anoda big word so....scoun...
weti?

Lukong

Scoundrel.

Ekambi

Yes. Na which wan dat?

Lukong

Scoundrel? Na man wey krokro and poor don finish i
all.

Ekambi

Me! krokro... poor...finish me kwatakwata! *(Making for
the cells)* I mus go broke dat Ghandi i banja now now so.
Wusai woman commot for kam talk for mi so?

Lukong

Lef one side for me make I kam finish am! *(Then pensively to
audience)* In life you acquire everything you possess. You only
have to be careful about people interrupting you each time you
are in the process of acquiring because some of those
interruptions can be hot...like the one we have just seen.
*(Enter Police Commissioner with Laura. Constables jump to hasty and confused
salute)*

Commissioner
(With commanding sternness)

This lady was here
to see her husband.

Both constables
(Saluting)

Yes Sa!

Commissioner

Has she?

Both constables
(Saluting again confusedly)

Yes Sa! No Sa!
(Commissioner and Laura gaze at them)

Lukong
(Pointing at Ekambi)

Him Sa! It was him!

150

Ekambi

Liar! Fat liar! Your neck. *(Clutching neck in demonstration)* Langa. You wanted all.

Commissioner

All what? *(No response)* Never mind. I will know soon enough. Open that cell. *(Both clamour towards cell knocking each other down in the process)* Ekambi, step your fat head back. *(Ekambi salutes and steps aside. Lukong opens cell and Ghandi emerges in chains)* Who put him in chains? *(Both Constables point accusingly at each other. Commissioner in controlled anger)* Ekambi, free him. *(Ekambi grudgingly bends and undoes chains)*

Ghandi

(To Commissioner)

Thank you, Sir.

Commissioner

My duty. And what were the circumstances of your arrest?

Ghandi

Kum & co. They turned my own wallet against me.

Commissioner

Kum and the wallet game again! That's how they rob innocent people around here. *(At Constables)* And these yams here know it. Out you go the two of you and don't return here without the Kum gang, which should be in under an hour. *(Lukong and Ekambi scurry out)* I'll leave you and your wife together while we wait for the gang.

Laura

We are very grateful, Sir.

Commissioner

My pleasure. I'll be back shortly.
(Exit Commissioner. Ghandi and Laura gaze at each other for some time, then fall into each other's arms)

Ghandi

(Poised at stage corner with Laura watching in admiration)
I am no scavenger that feeds on carrion. Ntonifor Ghandi whose groins spat me knew not the sight or smell of borrowed meat. He hunted. And not snails or lizards, but fully built

151

dear… and tiger, and lions on finer expeditions. I grew up in his footsteps. Laboured for my upkeep. Yet here I am. Thief in a marketplace. Thief of my own wallet, roped in a tyre. The world is standing on its head. Kum & co.
roam the streets, loot homes, shoot and stab, and retire everyday with blood and booty to their lair. They make no secret of their boast, for they have alliances in high places. Termites have eaten the foundations. Just a tap and all will crumble. Yet we boast of a home, solid enough to stand the tsunami. The clock is ticking for us. Ticking towards our last encounter with our crimes. *(Stentoriously)* Karma! Karma!

Laura

My dear husband, Innocent Sunday…

Ghandi

Not that one. Evil sits on his crooked nose like flies on carrion. The likes of him are today's cancer… he and his ugly stomach like an overflowing garbage can.

Laura

It will be good to do an ecography
of that his stomach.

Ghandi

The weight and stench
of the dirt
will blow up
house and machine!
(Enter Commissioner followed by Constables with Kum & co. in handcuffs)

Commissioner

(To confused protests and pleading from gang)
Lock them up! *(To Constables)* The two of you: three-month suspension without pay for collusion with robbers. And Disciplinary Council for the commanding officer. Mr Ghandi, you can return to your job and family. We apologize for the embarrassment.

Curtain

Scene 5

On Nonobit's farm.

(Workers in angry protest.)

Nonobit
(Holding up piece of paper)

My loan application.
Rejected!

Ewang

What was yours for?

Nonobit

Fertilizers. My crops are sick.

Ewang

You're even lucky you planted. Mine was for seeds.
My fields are bare.

Bine

With a deposit of 900.000 FCFA. I am denied a loan
of 25.000. All my chicks are dying. No feed.

Enegembole

The Farmers' Cooperative Scheme is fast turning into
the Farmers' Collective Grave.

Others
(In noisy protest)

It cannot be! It must not be!

Enegembole
(Seizing the initiative)

Calm! It cannot be! It must not
be! Each person is saying his own thing. But we need to
speak with one   voice. Unity is…

All

Str –e –ngth! Ye! Ye! Ye !

Enegembole

Quiet ! Unity is strength! If we are going to rescue the
Cooperative Scheme, what do we need?

All

(With grim purpose)

Unity!

Enegembole

Unity. Our money is used against us. Employed to quicken
our death. Today it's our crops and our chicks.
Tomorrow it will be our children. Then us.

All

(Confusedly)

My sweat! My money! God forbid! Heavens help!

Enegembole

Heavens help. You are right. But remember, heaven
helps only those who help themselves. Innocent Sunday
has planted his claws in our savings, bleeding them to
death. And he will not let go
easily. We need a farmers' delegate...a man with ....

All

(Cutting in with noisy happiness)

Not a man! No! No! A
woman! Enegembole! *(chanting)* Enege! Enege! Enege!

Enegembole

Thank you! Thank you! We are talking about leadership,
not entertainment. Somebody like Nonobit can be a good
delegate.

All

(Confusedly once again)

Nonobit! Enege! Why not Enege?
But why not Nonobit? Enege!....Nonobit!...me!...it can
also be me!...why not?

Enegembole

Calm. You see? Your mouth says one thing and your
heart says another. Picking a leader is not as easy as you
think. Since everybody wants to be the delegate,
we shall vote. *(All throw confused looks around)*. Vote.
Yes. We don't have the same idea of who should
represent us. My choice may not be your choice. So we
need to agree on one person.

Ewang

But how is that to be?

Nonobit

Yes, how?

Enegembole

I will tell you how. Sit down, all of you. *(All sit.)*
Now, who do we need?

Bine

(Putting up his hand to Enegembole's approval)

A farmers' delegate.

Enegembole

Good. We need a farmers' delegate. Are we all agreed?

All

Yes!

Enegembole

Right. Whose interest will he serve?

Ewang

(Putting up his hand to her approval)

Mine.

All

(Hushing him down confusedly)

Yours eh? You who?
See me this yam! And what about mine? And mine?

Enegembole

Enough! He has spoken his mind. The farmers'
delegate is not one man's property. He will represent
all of us and defend all our interests.

All

Aha! Yes! That's the way it should be!

Enegembole

Enough! Now, how many of us are here?

Bine

(Rising and counting and leaving himself out)

Three.

Nonobit

(Upbraiding him)

Count yourself too, foolish man.

Bine
(Taking count again this time including himself)

Four.

Enegembole

Good. That's our voting strength. You cannot carry
out a proper voting exercise without first of all
knowing the number of people who will vote.

Bine

It's like paying money for a girl before seeing her.

All
(In excited confusion)

Chei! That will be terrible!

Ewang
(Monopolizing the laughter)

Then she appears with a face
like pounded foofoo that has fallen on gravel.

Bine

With koni eyes and smelling like Tiko rubber factory. *(All catch
their necks as if to avoid throwing up)*

Enegembole

Enough! What do you take women for? The womb
that bore you! The sweat that feeds you! What do you
take women for, the bunch of you? This earth you
work is woman. Woman the crops you harvest.
Let woman frown and you will know no good days.
She holds your laughter in her palms, your sleep on
her shoulders, your manly groan between her laps.
(Men acquiesce confusedly) Let woman turn her back
and you count stars all night long. Woman is your
world, your all. *(Further noises from men)*

Nonobit
(Pointing angrily at Bine and Ewang)

This foolish two!
But I don't blame you. By the way, Ewang cannot
vote. He has not been long here with us.
He is not even from here.

Ewang
(Rising and challenging him)

Why? What do you
mean by that? I've not been long here. Here where?
And how long is long? And here from where even?

Enegembole

Enough! Ewang will vote. When it comes to work
you do not ask where he is from or how long he has
been here.

Bine

But Enege, you have been talking all the time. This
your sweet mouth that you are using on us like this,
will any of us have space to say anything again?

Enegembole

Why not? Have we started campaigning? When
campaign starts, all of us will have the same time to
convince the voters.

Ewang
(Rising and pointing spitefully at Nonobit)

We are in this
one's farm. Will he not think we should all vote him for that
reason? He is already even saying I should not vote.

Enegembole

We are not voting for a farm. All of us have farms
and houses. We are voting for a delegate,
a person who can do the job waiting to be done.

Nonobit

We should wait for the sun to go down before we vote.

Ewang

Crook! No! No! You want me to go home and then you
remain behind and play hanky panky.

Bine

Ewang is right. Our homes are far, so we should vote
now so that all of us can see
how the thing goes.

Enegembole

The voting will take place now when the sun is still up and we are
seeing our faces. No corner corner palaver.

157

Bine

Who are the candidates?

Ewang

(Putting up his hand to Enegembole's approval)

I nominate Enegembole.

Enegembole

I accept.

Bine

And I Nonobit.

Nonobit

I accept.

Enegembole

Bine, now that you are not running, you will oversee the
exercise.

Bine

I will. Each one of you will have twenty seconds to
convince us. Nonobit, you will begin.

Nonobit

(Moving to forestage and addressing audience)

We formed the Farmers' Cooperative Scheme as a
support fund. But a wolf has seized it. He pays no heed to our
cry. He never visits our farms. He never mingles with us. He
knows only our money, not us. The farmers are ruined. Their
farms are wretched. Hunger devours their families. We must
chase out the wolf. Vote for…

Bine

(Cutting in)

Thank you. Your time is up. We shall listen
to Enegembole.

Enegembole

(Stepping forward to a spirited performance).

I will not say much. *(To audience).* Is Innocent Sunday
innocent? Is he a saint or a rogue? Is he for us
or against us? Shall we praise him or hang him? Thank you!

Bine

Thank you both. *(To audience).* We shall all vote by
show of hand. Those who want Nonobit to be our
Farmers' Delegate should put up their hands. Ewang,

158

count them. *(Ewang counts and gives the total).* Those who think it should be Enegembole should put up their hands. Ewang, count. *(Ewang counts and reaches a higher total).* My dear friends, as you yourselves can see, Enegembole has won the elections. Does anyone challenge the results? *(Silence)* So Enegembole is our new Delegate. *(All congratulate the winner).*

Curtain

Scene 6

Innocent Sunday's office
(Accountant before him.)

Mr. Sunday
Laura.

Accountant
Mrs. Ghandi, Sir.

Mr. Sunday
As you please. The latest transactions.

Accountant
Right, Sir. By midday we had recorded deposits
of 4 million seven hundred thousand. You gave
orders that 4 million be sent off to your Swiss account
immediately, which was done. Our figures now stand
at 2 million seven hundred thousand.
(Enter Enegembole in militant mood)

Enegembole
Did I hear well? 2 million seven hundred thousand.
That's less money than I alone have put in this
scheme.

Mr. Sunday
(Derisively)
Who's that one and how did she find
herself in my office?

Enegembole
Never mind who I am. You will know soon enough.

Mr. Sunday
(With mounting irritation)
But who the hell are you?

Enegembole
You do well to talk about hell: one of us belongs
there.

Mr. Sunday
(To Accountant)
Let the guards get this filthy thing out
of my presence!

Enegembole

Thanks for the compliment. Farmers are filthy things.

Mr. Sunday

Just that. If you are a farmer… and I see you are
One, then you are in the wrong place. This is an office..
the office of a Bank Manager, not a farm, so out you go
before I throw you out myself.

Enegembole

(With disdainful calm)

Mr Bank Manager, I am a farmer
as you can see, and the Delegate of all the farmers.
I am here to see into the running of our Scheme.

Accountant

(With visible relief)

My sister! Come and help me!

Mr. Sunday

(Scolding Accountant)

Mind your words. What help do
you need around here? *(To Enegembole)* And you! Whoever you
say you are, you are in the wrong place. I know of no such thing
as a farmers' delegate. I don't treat with farmers here. I handle
money!

Enegembole

(To audience laughing)

He doesn't treat with farmers.
He handles money. *(To Mr. Sunday sharply).* Whose money?

Mr. Sunday

What effrontery!

Accountant

(With emphatic calmness to Mr. Sunday)

She has asked a simple question, Sir. Answer her.

Mr. Sunday

(To Accountant)

You face instant dismissal unless you
come back to your senses. And quickly!

Enegembole

She is not the one to come back to her senses.

Accountant

My sister!

Mr. Sunday
(Angrily)

What is all this sister business about? We are
not in a convent here. We are in a bank.

Accountant

Precisely, Sir, so answer her question.

Enegembole

My sister, wait. *(Ferrets bag)*. Take and see. *(Hands
passbook over)*.

Accountant
(In amazed admiration)

My sister! 3 million five
hundred thousand.

Enegembole

That's my money in this Scheme. And I want 2 million
seven hundred and five thousand as I am standing here
now like this!

Mr. Sunday

Did I hear well? Two million seven hundred and five
thousand. That's more money than the bank has.

Enegembole
(With studied emphasis)

We are in a bank, not on a
farm.

Accountant
(In relief)

My sister oh!

Enegembole

And talking about banks, they are not airports:
money does not fly off from them. They are not
whirlpools: money does not sink in them. They are not blast
furnaces: money does not burn up in them. They are not
cataracts: they do not pulp money.

Accountant

And talking still about banks, they produce money,
they don't empty money; they attract money, they don't
repel money; they yield dividends, they don't spin losses;
they protect money, they don't squander money.

Enegembole

My sister oh! *(To Mr Sunday, with stern determination)*. Two million
seven hundred and five thousand frs. It is the farmer talking.

Accountant

To the Banker.

Mr. Sunday

(To Accountant)

I have warned you against your stupid
utterances.

Accountant

Things are not always what they seem ... Sir.

Mr. Sunday

Enough of it! *(To Enegembole, with unflagging
haughtiness)* We will ask you, in your own interest,
to take the shortest way out of here.

Enegembole

You must be joking. I am here for money, my money,
and I will have it... here and now.

Mr. Sunday

Guards! *(Guards rush in)* Out with her. Get her out
and far.
(Guards raise Enegembole shoulder high to her noisy protest)

Curtain

Scene 7

In Nonobit's farm
Work in progress. Enter Enegembole in triumphant mood.

Enegembole

Give that work a break, all of you. *(Heads rise in her direction)* What do you labour for?

Nonobit

The Farmers' Cooperative Scheme.

All

Why? Yes.

Enegembole

Dump your tools, if so.

All

Eh?

Enegembole

As I say.

Nonobit

The Scheme…what of it?

Bine

And our money in it?

Enegembole

Dead. Do you hear? Dead. Innocent Sunday has cut a hole under the accounts: not a franc stays.

All

Not a franc? *(Scattering out in confused anger)*.

Enegembole

(Harshly)

Back here, all of you! Where are they going to? *(All return)*. Now listen. You are all as rich as you are standing here, me inclusive. The Scheme is robbed. Plundered. Laid fallow. Dead. No carcass left even for the vultures. But that will not be the end of it. Sunday must account for our money.

All

(Confusedly)

Yes…yes…yes… to the last franc.

Enegembole

Tomorrow we shall storm the place.

All

(In excited confusion).

Tomorrow. Quick. No. Today.
Now. Let's have him now. This very minute.
(Enter Mrs. Ghandi)

Enegembole

Hold! The Accountant ! *(Expectant silence).*

Mrs Ghandi

I greet you all.

Nonobit

(Indignantly)

Woman, is it true what we hear?

Bine

Our money. All gone?

Mrs. Ghandi

Just as your Delegate reported to you.

All

(In deafening commotion)

God forbid! It shall not be!
Not my money!

Mrs Ghandi

Hear me! Calm!

Enegembole

All this noise will not help. Let's hear the Accountant.
It's certainly not for nothing that she has come.

Mrs. Ghandi

You speak well, my sister. My dear friends,
the Farmers' Cooperative Scheme is dead.

All

Eh?

Mrs. Ghandi

Yes, dead.

All

Eh? With all its holdings?

Mrs. Ghandi

With all its holdings.
Mr Sunday asked me to send the
money to his Swiss account.

Nonobit
(Pointing)

That place where money goes and never comes back?

Mrs. Ghandi

Yes.
But do you think I did as he said?

All

We wonder.

Mrs. Ghandi

No. In addition to being a woman, I also have a
head.

All
(Noisily)

We can see it. And a beautiful one too.

Mrs Ghandi

Sense, know-how, not beauty. I said to myself: this is
the farmers' sweat and no jot of it will disappear, much
less cross the ocean to I do not know which safe haven
for rogues. And so I used the money to create a
new home for your money called the Farmers Trust.
That's the new bank where all your money is kept. *(All
break into dance of celebration round her.)*

Enegembole

Stop. We have heard, or have we not?

All

Not heard? We have!

Mrs. Ghandi

I forgot one thing. The idea to start the Farmers' Trust
was given to me by my husband.

All
(Chanting)

Ghandi! Sende! Sende!

166

Enegembole

Enough. What do we do with the bank?

Nonobit

Our bank, you mean?

Enegembole

Our bank, yes. What do we do with it?

Bine

Sende Ghandi. He shall be the Manager.

All

Sende! Manager! Manager!

Ewang

(Pointing excitedly at Mrs Ghandi)

And she!

Accountant! Yes, she shall be the Accountant.

Bine

Not only Accountant. Accountant-in-Chief!

All

(Dancing round)

Approved. Yes. Ghandi for Manager!

Mrs! Ghandi for Accountant. Accountant-in-chief!

(Enter Ghandi to triumphant reception)

Curtain

Scene 8

In Innocent Sunday's office

He is at his table, looking thoroughly pleased with himself. Bells Accountant in.

Mr. Sunday
(In admiration as she walks in)
Ever so beautiful!

Accountant
I'm flattered, Sir.

Mr. Sunday
Beauty is meant to be admired, you know.

Accountant
(Dutifully)
Especially by those who know what beauty
is. Like you.

Mr. Sunday
(Encouraged by Accountant's receptiveness)
Yes…yes… Laura…eh…Mrs Ghandi.

Accountant
You can call me Laura, Sir.

Mr. Sunday
(Smiling invitingly)
And you call me Sunday?

Accountant
One bit at a time, Sir. By tomorrow, surely, I
should be able to. There's some business, I think.

Mr. Sunday
Sure. Our account. How is it doing?

Accountant
Which of them, Sir?

Mr. Sunday
Why, the Swiss one.
Is there any reason to worry about this one here?

Accountant
No, Sir, of course not. The Swiss account is doing

exceptionally well. In fact, just this morning the
Manager called to congratulate us for the regularity
and power of our deposits. He said we ranked among his top
five clients in terms of regularity, and second only to one Sheik
from the Arab Emirate in terms of volume of deposit. Let me
go for the records, Sir.

Mr. Sunday

No! No! Never mind about the records. *You* are the
records, Laura. *(Rising   and pacing the stage)* You see,
money well earned must be well spent. That's just what we will
do, you and me, Laura. You can return to your office. I'll call you
back in an instant. *(Exit Accountant to overt ogling by him.*
Then in jubilant soliloquy) Power. If this is not power, what
else is? All the power is in money.
Money is power. *(At audience)* You see her? She has
become mine. My money has conquered her. She cannot
wait. I cannot wait. Mrs. Ghandi here, Mrs. Ghandi there.
Finished. Which right-thinking woman will prefer a
(emphatically) wretch in prison to the millions…no…not
millions…it cannot be millions only…to the billions…yes…
billions I am worth? Laura is clever. *(Touching his nose)*
Money has a fragrance which no human will can resist.
(Calls Accountant in ostentatiously. Accountant comes running
in with mock readiness) Sit down. Here. On my laps.

Accountant

(With feigned politeness)
Not right away, Sir. There will be time for that.

Mr. Sunday

Surely. Our hotel suite in Geneva will be a better
setting. We need to arrange a trip to Sweetzerland. Have
you ever flown?

Accountant

Never, Sir.

Mr. Sunday

Then hurry with the arrangements. Ever spent the night in a
continental suite?

Accountant

No, Sir.

Mr. Sunday

Then hurry with the arrangements. You said our banker
called this morning, did you?

Accountant

Yes, he did, to congratulate us.

Mr. Sunday

The number. Let me have it. I want him to make some
Transfer to us here for local preparations... a few suits
for myself...and for you some dresses and jewellery.

Accountant

Let me have your phone, Sir. *(Dials number on cellular and
hands phone back to Mr. Sunday)* It's ringing.

Mr. Sunday

(Holds phone excitedly. Gestures to Laura as voice comes on)
Helo! Yes! My name? Innocent... Innocent Sunday.
(Blocking phone with hand) He says I should give him a
split second. *(Returning to phone)* Helo!
That I should repeat my name? I'm one of your top five
customers. It's my name you want? Sunday. Innocent
Sunday. *(Drops phone)* Says he's going down to the
archives. That my name is not in their updated data bank.
The archives must be the special place where names of the
top five are held, surely for security reasons. You've been
doing a wonderful job, Laura.

Accountant

Thank you, Sir. I owe you that duty. Sir, can I just step out
while you are waiting for the call and see to a few things?

Mr. Sunday

Sure, sure. I hope you are not on your way to that scoundrel
in prison.

Accountant

How on earth? I've forgotten even his name.
(Exit)

Mr. Sunday

(Consulting his watch with some impatience)

Are those archives on the moon? These Swiss banks. When it comes to receiving your money they are quick. But to give it back to you is a problem. Ever since he said I should give him some time. I will have to point this out to him. Customers take priority in these things. If I don't put my money there he will be out of work. He has to know that and treat me tidily. I hope interest is accruing. Otherwise I'll withdraw all my money. The interest rate has to be good, something like 12%. That's what you put your money in the bank for. It has to grow, yield dividends. That's how you tell a good bank. The money must be handy and plentiful. *(Consulting watch again)* That man must be dead. How? Is he a feyman? Let it not be that he is a 419 oh! These people like this you can never trust them. And Laura too, where is she gone to? She should be here following this business up. She knows where she kept the money. Maybe those her bankers know only her. *(Enter Accountant with Sende Ghandi and Commissioner. Wiping his eyes in disbelief)* Why? No! What is this? What is all this supposed to mean? *(Pointing hysterically at Sende Ghandi)* You…you…what are you doing here? You are in prison. Go away! Laura…the arrangements. Make them… quick! quick! quick! We must leave for Sweetzerland, now, right now. The hotel suite, my milli…billi… *(Reaches for Laura Ghandi but is stopped by Commissioner)*

Commissioner

Calm, Mr. Innocent Sunday. You will go on your trip. That's why I am here. You've been preparing for it right from the day you became Manager of the Farmers' Co-operative Scheme. *(To a crestfallen Innocent Sunday)* You are under arrest, Sir. *(Commissioner marches Innocent Sunday out as he throws a last guilty look at audience. The Ghandis wave at him as he departs)*

Curtain. End.